The Christian Life Series

By REV. F. B. MEYER, B. A.

THE SHEPHERD PSALM

CHRISTIAN LIVING

THE PRESENT TENSES OF
THE BLESSED LIFE

THE FUTURE TENSES OF
THE BLESSED LIFE

16mo, each, 50 cents

FLEMING H. REVELL COMPANY
PUBLISHERS

Christian Living

By F. B. MEYER, B. A.

AUTHOR OF "THE SHEPHERD PSALM,"
"OLD TESTAMENT HEROES," ETC.

We thus judge . . . that they which live should not
henceforth live unto themselves, but unto Him which died for
them and rose again. — ii Cor. v: 14, 15.

CHICAGO   NEW YORK   TORONTO
FLEMING H. REVELL COMPANY
PUBLISHERS OF EVANGELICAL LITERATURE

248
M57C

5698

The Lakeside Press
R. R. DONNELLEY & SONS COMPANY
CHICAGO

PREFACE.

THESE chapters contain the essence of Addresses delivered at several Conferences and Missions, in which they have been wonderfully used to the quickening of the children of God.

Looked at in this form, they seem as unlikely to produce life as the rod which was laid in vain on the face of the dead child (2 Kings iv. 31). Yet may He who caused the rod of Aaron to bud and bear fruit graciously bless these words after like manner; and use them to answer some of the questions which are being so eagerly asked on all sides, as to the attainment of a nobler ideal of Christian Living.

CONTENTS.

CHRISTIAN LIVING.

I.

The Appropriation of Christ.

"Put ye on the Lord Jesus Christ."—*Romans xiii. 14.*

AT the beginning of the Christian life, for the most part at least, we try to *imitate* Jesus Christ. There is Scriptural warrant for our doing so. And the time will never come when we may not look up to Him as our model and ideal, with that eager, longing gaze which must exert something of a transforming influence. But if this be all, we shall find our Christian life one of unutterable disappointment and sorrow. The infinite beauty and glory of our ideal must ever distance our noblest efforts, as the inaccessible heights of the

Jungfrau, clad in untrodden snows, rise higher and ever higher above the traveller as he approaches them along the valley at their foot.

In a railway carriage recently I was attracted by the earnest look on the face of a young man who was reading "The Imitation of Christ." Some kinship of spirit drew me to his side, and the conversation naturally opened by a reference to the holy meditations of the almost unknown saint, which has become part of the household literature of the Church. Without depreciating that precious manual of the holy life, I ventured to suggest that "imitation" alone was insufficient for the purpose we had in view; and that there was a more excellent way.

Years ago, when a lad at school, there was failure in my attempts to imitate with clumsy fingers the smooth copper-plate at the head of my copy-book nor was there better success in the cadeavor to imitate the finished drawing placed upon the easel; and the captain of the school could throw cricket-ball and hammer for almost as many yards, as the slender arms of his imitator could throw them feet. Yes, and as year after year I have tried to imitate the matchless glories of Jesus Christ, there has been the same weary sense of failure, beneath which heart and hope have sunk down baffled and disappointed.

There is another word, which carries with it the inspiration of a new hope, and speaks of the possibilities of faith —the word APPROPRIATION. Let us not be content with the effort to imitate Christ; let us appropriate Him, as the flowers of spring and the fruits of autumn appropiate the properties of the sap and dew and balmy air, and all the glorious forces that lie hid in sunbeams.

This thought is Scriptural. What is it but another way of expressing the Apostle's exhortation to "put on the

Lord Jesus Christ"? (Rom. xiii. 14.) In Him, by the good pleasure of the Father, all fulness dwells, that we might receive of it grace upon grace; and that reception is but another term for appropriation. In giving us His Son, the Father hath given unto us all things that pertain unto life and godliness; but that gracious provision avails us nothing until we claim and appropriate it by a living faith. The promises are all ours: but they are vain until we lay upon them the hand of appropriating proprietorship; and, as heirs, enter upon our inheritance. All true faith must have in it this thought of appropriation. We first know by hearing what are our glorious privileges and rights. Then we reckon that the record is true. And, finally, we begin to use that which has been so freely given. Like the pilgrim-saints of olden days, "we are persuaded of them, and embrace them." (Heb. xi. 13.)

This thought is also confirmed by experience. A little group of earnest men were gathered not long ago around a fire, eagerly discussing the methods of a holy life, and reciting their own experiences of the grace of God. One had recently entered upon the gladness of a life of entire consecration, and spoke fervently of his new-found joys. But when his story was told, a venerable clergyman expressed his disappointment at an experience which was only negative, and told so little of the positive side of the appropriation of Christ.

Years before, when engaged in a gathering of unruly and noisy children, he had been suddenly driven to claim from the Saviour the gift of his own gentle patience, in the words, "Thy patience, Lord!" And instantly so divine a calm filled his spirit that he realized that he had made a great discovery. And from that moment he had retained the extremes of his brief petition, in-

serting between them the grace, the lack
of which was hurrying him to sin.   In
moments of weakness, "Thy strength,
Lord!" or in moments of conscious
strength, "Thy humility, Lord!" When
assailed by unholy suggestions, "Thy
purity, Lord!" or when passing through
deep waters of trial, "Thy resignation
and restfulness, Lord!" What is this
but a living example of the appropriation of Christ?

*This thought would light up the darkest,
saddest life.* We sadly chide ourselves
for our failures; and yet we are op-
pressed by the weary consciousness that
we are all too likely to repeat them.
We catch glimpses of ideals in the lives
of others, and in our own happier moments, that only mock us. We fail to
adorn the Gospel of God our Saviour
in all things, because we lack the materials for the beautiful garments of our
array. And all this because we do not
realize that all of Jesus is for us; only

waiting for us to appropriate it with exceeding joy.

Jesus Christ is an Armory, in which hang armour for defence, and weapons for attack. Happy is he who has learned to enter the sacred arsenal, to gird on the breast-plate and helmet, and to lay his hand to spear and sword! Christ is a Banqueting-house, in which the tables groan beneath the weight of all that is needed for the supply of appetite and the gratification of taste. Happy is he who makes free of the rich provision, and comes to it whenever he needs! Christ is a Surgery, stored with all manner of restoratives and blessed elixirs; nor lacks an ointment for every wound, a cordial for every faintness, a remedy for every disease. Happy is he who is well-skilled in heavenly pharmacy, and knoweth how to avail himself of his healing virtues: Christ is the Jewel-room, in which the graces of the Christian are held in strong and safe keeping. Happy is he who knows which is the key to the massive doors, so that he can go in and out at his will, and array himself in "whatsoever things are lovely, and whatsoever things are of good report!" With burning words like these the saintly heart expatiates on the fulness of Christ. But, after all, how inadequate the words are to express all the rapture, the strength, the grace, which become the spending-money of the man who has learnt to appropriate the Lord Jesus! He moves from the attic into comfortable apartments. He becomes a first-class traveller by the most luxurious route. He no longer laments his leanness; but cries with the ring of a new hope, "I can do all things through Christ which strengtheneth me."

It is difficult—nay, impossible—to employ words sufficiently emphatic, or forcible, to enforce this habit of Christ-appropriation on Christian hearts. Suffice it to say that it would be as life

from the dead for many who read these
lines, and whose life has been a series
of disappointments. Let us work it out
in one or two directions, as suggested
by the Apostle when he says: "Of
Him are ye in Christ Jesus, who of God
is made unto us wisdom, and righteousness, and sanctification, and redemption." (1 Cor. i. 30.)   Let us

I. APPROPRIATE CHRIST AS OUR WISDOM.

Many true Christains find it difficult
to know the will of God.   They long to
do it, if only they knew it; but it is hidden from their eyes.   "Should I move
to another town?" "Should I take such
a step in business?"   "Should I enter
into such a partnership, or ally myself
with such an enterprise?"   "Should I
embark in this new branch of Christian
activity?"   Such questions are constantly arising and pressing for an answer in all our lives; and as they do so
they excite the instant inquiry, "Lord,

what wilt Thou have me to do?"

But how may we know God's will? That is not always easy. Yet the difficulty is not in Him. He does not wish us to grope painfully in the dark. Nay, He is ever giving us many signs and hints as to the way we should take, too delicate to be perceived by the coarse eye of sense, but clear enough to those who are divested of self-will and pride, and only anxious to know and do the holy and acceptable and perfect will of God.

It is a mistake to seek a sign from heaven; to run from counsellor to counsellor; to cast a lot; or to trust to some chance coincidence. Not that God may not reveal His will thus; but because it is hardly the behaviour of a child with its Father. There is a more excellent way. Let the heart be quieted and stilled in the presence of God; weaned from all earthly distractions and worldly ambitions. Let the voice of the Son

of God hush into perfect rest the storms
that sweep the lake of the inner life,
and ruffle its calm surface. Let the
whole being be centred on God Himself. And then, remembering that all
who lack wisdom are to ask it of God,
and that Jesus Christ is already made
unto us wisdom, let us quietly appropriate Him, in that capacity, by faith;
and then go forward, perhaps not conscious of any increase of wisdom, or
able to see far in front; but sure that
we shall be guided, as each new step
must be taken, or word spoken, or de-
cision made. It is an immense help in
any difficulty to say, "I take thee, Lord
Jesus, as my wisdom," and to do the
next thing, nothing doubting; assured
that He will not permit those who trust
in Him to be ashamed.

II. LET US APPROPRIATE CHRIST AS OUR
RIGHTEOUSNESS.

It is not necessary to convince the
readers of these lines that they need a

righteousness, in whose stainless white they may stand accepted before the Holy Father. That, alas! is but too apparent. Conscious of our nakedness and sin, we once sought to establish our own righteousness, stitching together the fig-leaves, which died as we plucked them, and became sere and shrivelled. But since then we have submitted ourselves to the righteousness of God, which is by faith. There is often, however, an apparent doubt in Christian hearts as to their relation to that righteousness; and they do not realize that, whether they feel it not, it is, nevertheless, covering them, in all its radiant beauty; for in the thought of God, every believer is arrayed in the beauteous dress of the Saviour's finished work. "It is UPON all them that believe." (Rom. iii. 22.) There is only one kind of faith, and directly it is exercised, though amid many doubts and fears, the believer is justified, accepted in the

Beloved, and accounted not only as forgiven, but as righteous in the sight of
God. This is so, whether it be realized
or not.

The first moment of faith is the time
when we begin to appropriate the righteousness of Christ. At first it is with
trembling hands that we gird ourselves
in the dress that cost our Lord so much.
We fear, as we enter the most holy
place, and stand where angels worship;
but, as the days pass on, and we learn
more of its efficiency, its adaptation to
our need, and its preciousness in the
sight of God, we become more assured
of our position, and notwithstanding repeated failures in the past, the misgiv-
ings of nature, and the taunts of hell,
we have boldness to enter into that
which is within the vail.

Jesus Christ has been made to us
righteousness by God; but He needs to
be appropriated by faith when we are
first convinced of sin, and ever after,

when conscious of our worthlessness
and guilt. How triumphant the ejacu-
lation, "Jesus, I flee unto Thee to hide
me; I appropriate Thee as my righteousness before God!"

"I will greatly rejoice in the Lord,
my soul shall be joyful in my God: for
He hath clothed me with the garments
of salvation, He hath covered me with
the robe of righteousness."

III. Let us appropriate Christ as our Sanctification.

Sanctification is separation—separation from sin; separation to God, to the
point of devotion. There often arises
before us the vision of a devoted life;
such a life as Jesus lived, whose only
thought was to do the will of God. To
recognize God as the sole source of holiness. To lean on Him, and to listen for
His voice within the heart as the sole
and sufficient guide. To live apart from
the restless aims and fretting ambitions

of men. To be separate from sin—holy, harmless, and without rebuke. To keep ever in touch with God and His thoughts and aims. To obey him at all hazards and costs. To be the channel through which the river of God may flow down into earth's desert places, making them rejoice and blossom—ah, what an ideal is here!

Yet at first this ideal mocks us sorely. It is high, we cannot attain unto it. And we shall be beaten by repeated failures until we learn the secret, which is just now our chosen theme. Apart from that, there is nothing for us, but sadly to renounce the bright vision as impossible; though perhaps reserved for saintly hearts which spend their time in cloistered piety.

But it is brought within the range of the humblest and weakest disciple, who renounces all hope of realizing it through nature's efforts, and who appropriates Christ in his all-sufficiency. Trust the

Holy Spirit to work in you a perpetual remembrance of the Lord Jesus; and then avail yourself of Him in all His offices and work. And amongst other aspects, be sure to appropriate Him as your sanctification. When tempted to cross the line of separation, or to relax the energy of your devotion, look upward, and say, "Be thou to me in fact that which the Father has already made Thee, in possibility and by right, my Sanctification."

IV. LET US APPROPRIATE CHRIST AS OUR REDEMPTION.

We have been redeemed from the curse of the law, because He was made a curse for us. But we long to be redeemed from the power of sin. "The good we would, we do not; the evil we would not, we do." And this longing shall be met; because it would not be like our God to leave us to the mercy of the strong Pharaoh-like foes, which have made us serve under cruel bondage for so long. He must come down to deliver us. Ah, what joyful news it is that He has done so, and has provided a sufficient deliverance in Jesus.

But this redemption waits our appropriation, as the flowers of spring await the hand of the flower-girl; or as the deliverance wrought for the Jews by Mordecai awaited their personal action, which made it their own. From this moment give up your strivings and endeavors, and take Christ as your deliverance from all the sins which have broken your peace, and cursed your joy. When the oppressor approaches you; when the old habit seeks to assert itself; when easily besetting sin begins to weave its snare about you, or suddenly to assail—then look up to the Saviour, and say, "I appropriate Thee as my redemption in this my hour of need!"

A lady travelling in the Southern States, after President Lincoln had proclaimed the freedom of the slaves, found a black woman, who was acting as a slave, because she did not know that her race was free. She had heard rumors, which her owner and others had denounced as lies. But as soon as she knew that she was free, she appropriated her freedom, and went forth into liberty. Let it be clearly understood that the Son has made us free, who bear His name; let us avail ourselves of our right; and go forth into the glorious liberty of the sons of God.

This is the secret, then, of a glad and victorious life, unshadowed by cloud or defeat: Jesus Christ for all who believe; awaiting only the appropriation of the most trembling hand stretched out towards Him in expectation of faith.

It is a goodly land which the Lord our God giveth us in which scarceness and penury are unknown. Let us not linger on the threshold, but go in to possess it with songs of thanksgiving.

II.

Christ's Proprietorship.

"Whose I am, and Whom I Serve."—*Acts xxvii. 23.*

IN the "SONG OF SONGS, which is Solomon's," there is a beautiful gradation
of expression, which significantly illus-
trates the successive steps in the experience of the soul.   Thrice does the
bride speak of the Bridegroom in similar
terms; but in each case there is a slight
alteration in the phraseology, which
speaks volumes of her deepening character, and truer attitude towards Him.

"My Beloved is mine, and I am His."
(Song of Solomon ii. 16.)   "I am my
Beloved's, and my Beloved is mine."
(vi. 3.)   "I am my Beloved's, and His
desire is toward me."   (vii. 10.)

At first she lays the chief stress on the thought that all her Beloved was hers, and that she had a right to employ concerning Him the appropriating pronoun *My;* it was only a secondary consideration that she was also *His*.

But as her thought ran on, she changed the relative place of the two clauses of the sentence, and laid her primal emphasis not on her appropriation of Him, but on his proprietorship of her: "I am His."

And, lastly, this conception so filled her mind that she had no thought of her side of the matter, and was altogether absorbed in the happy consciousness that she belonged utterly, and for ever, to the object of her supreme and adoring love.

This is also the history of each scholar in the school of grace. We begin by calculating how much there is in Christ for us. We appropriate His fulness, and count ourselves millionaires in His

wealth.   And there is no wrong or harm
in this.   But, as the days pass on, we
realize that there is a yet profounder truth
on which this rests; and to have *that* is
to have in addition all that Christ can
be and do for the soul which clings to
Him—as the limpet to the rock on
which the long line of waves breaks,
with boom of thunder and clouds of
spray, without detaching it from its
hold.   We begin by saying, *Christ is
mine:* we go on to say, *I am His.* We pass
from the appropriation of Christ by us
to the proprietorship of us by Christ.
And this is surely a happier and better
standing-ground: because the hand,
which appropriates only, may become
numbed and tired; but that which is
locked in the hand of Christ, in the
tight grasp of ownership, can never be
withdrawn.

Did you, my Christian reader, ever
realize the conception that you are absolutely Christ's?   You may not own it:

you may not live beneath its power:
nay, you may seek to cast the thought
aside; as Onesimus, who, when he fled
from Ephesus to hide himself, truant that
he was, in the slums of Rome, tried to
forget the claims which Philemon, his
master, had over him, by right of purchase. All this you may do: and yet,
in spite of all, you are as much Christ's
property as any slave would be the
chattel of the man who had paid down
his price in the market, or who had
received him as part of the family
estate by right of inheritance.

And not only are *you* the property of
Christ; but all you are and have is His
also. The master owns not only the
slave, but all the proceeds of his toils;
and all the personal or other property
which he may acquire. The hapless
serf can point to nothing as his; all is
his master's. He is but a steward,
bound to account for the way in which
every coin is expended; at the best per-

mitted to deduct from the general proceeds of the estate only a bare sufficiency for his personal maintenance; but expected to forward all the rest to his master, or expend it on such interests as he may direct. This is our rightful position with respect to Christ. Paul was proud to call himself the bond-slave of Jesus Christ. He chose as his motto the immortal words (badge of a slavery which does not degrade, but enobles all who bend beneath its yoke), "Whose I am, and whom I serve."

I. CHRIST'S PROPRIETORSHIP RESTS ON
MANY GROUNDS.

We are His *by Creation:* His image and superscription have been stamped upon every lineament of our face, though almost obliterated as the effigy of the sovereign from a well-worn coin. "It is He that hath made us, and His we are."

We are His *by Purchase:* for never was slave more certainly acquired by

silver and gold than we have been
bought by His precious blood. "Ye are
not your own, ye are bought with a
price, wherefore glorify God in your
body and in your spirit, which are His."

We are His *by Deed of Gift:* for the
Father has given to Him all who shall
come to Him; and it is impossible to
believe that donation could be of anything less than our whole being. When
God gave us, He gave all of us.

We are His *by Conquest:* for the Man-
soul of our inner nature has opened to
Him her gates, unable longer to resist;
and, even though He be not as yet re-
cognized in all her environs, there is
no doubt that He is her rightful Lord
and King.

Ah! it is impossible to escape the
fact, that in the thought of God, and
according to the rights of the case, we
are the absolute property of Jesus Christ,
our Lord: and that he thinks much of
that fact, is evident in the frequent re-

ferences of His High-priestly prayer
(John xvii.), though we, alas! are too
forgetful of His claims.

II.　THE ACT OF CONSECRATION CONSISTS
　　IN THE RECOGNITION OF CHRIST'S AB-
　　SOLUTE PROPRIETORSHIP.

Men often ask and wonder what that
consecration is to which they are urged.
They suppose that it is something altogether over and beyond what is expected from ordinary Christians.　But
this is a profound mistake.　Consecration is simply giving Christ His own,
and restoring stolen property to its
rightful owner.　Consecration is to give
to Christ by choice that which is His
by indefeasible right; but which He
will not snatch from any one.

The men of Israel were David's by
God's appointment; but they could not
rest content until they had swum the Jor-
dan at its flood, and had fallen at the feet
of their rightful king, crying, "**Thine**

are we, David; and on thy side, thou
son of Jesse." (1 Chron. xii. 1–18.)
Should we be content without saying as
much to our Saviour, Jesus?

Of course we all in a general way recognize Christ's ownership. "We are
His people, and the sheep of his pas-
ture." But we must do it in a particular
and personal sense. We must crown
Him King of our hearts and lives by our
own glad choice. We must bring the
whole of our nature and life under His
direct control. We must be willing that
His will should be as supreme, and as
universally honored, in us, as it is in His
own bright home. We must come to
the point of saying something like this:
"Lord Jesus, I am Thine by right; forgive me for having lived so long as if I
were my own. I now gladly recognize
that Thou hast a rightful claim on all I
have and am; I want to live as Thine
from henceforth; and I do solemnly at
this hour give myself to Thee, by my own

glad choice: Thine entirely: Thine in
life and death: Thine forever."

III. THERE ARE A FEW CAUTIONS AND
DIRECTIONS NECESSARY IN THIS ACT
OF CONSECRATION.

(1) The act of consecration is the
taking-up of an attitude, which must
never be renounced; or if it is lost for a
moment, it must instantly be resumed,
with prayer for forgiveness and for
cleansing. But this is only possible
through the gracious aid of the Eternal
Spirit, through whom the Lord Jesus
offered Himself without spot to God;
and through whom alone, we shall be
able to take up and maintain this sacred
attitude.

(2) As the light grows we shall become increasingly aware of new depart-
ments of our heart and life, that were
not consciously included in our first
glad act of surrender. But as they come
to view, we must hand them also into

the governorship of the King. We must
send them on, as we might send on the
loose sheets of a book to a friend, who
had already taken away the bulk.

(3) There is no reason, in the nature
of the case, why the children of God
should not become consecrated from the
very moment of conversion. It should
be the normal state of Christians. And
with many it is so. Redeemed from
eternal death, they instantly give themselves to their Deliverer, as those alive
from the dead. But with most this is
not the case. And so it is necessary, at
some future period of their lives, when
the claims of Christ suddenly break on
them, that they should come to the
definite point of self-surrender.

(4) It matters little when, and how,
we do it; whether by speech, or in
writing; whether alone, or in company.
But we must not be content with a vague
desire. There should be a definite act,
at a given moment of time, when we

shall gladly sign, and seal, and confess,
that we are His. (Isaiah xliv. 5.)

(5) Sometimes we may feel unable
to GIVE all; but we are willing that He
should TAKE all. . This is equally acceptable to Him. And is it not a better
and more scriptural way of putting the
truth? For we might be troubled by
grievous questionings, as to whether we
had really given *all*, or whether there
were not some fatal flaw in our act. But
if the question is simply one of His
taking—or of our being willing for Him
to take—entire possession; so ,that
every imagination is cast down, every
thought brought into captivity, and our
wills moulded into harmony with His:
then rough places are made smooth,
and crooked ones straight. This is the
charm of Miss Havergal's Consecration
Hymn; its key-word is—TAKE!

(6) The ACT OF CONSECRATION is can-
celled by one reserve. To give ninety-
nine parts and to withhold the hun-

dredth undoes the whole transaction
because in that one piece of reserve the
whole of the self-life entrenches itself,
defying Him. It may seem impossible
to renounce that one thing; but in clinging to it, you forego for ever all right
to His blessed fulness. The electrician
cannot charge your body with electricity, while a single thread connects you
with the ground, and breaks the com-
pleteness of your insulation. The physician cannot undertake your case whilst
you conceal one symptom, or yourself
seek to effect a cure in one particular.
The Lord Jesus cannot fully save you
whilst there is one point of controversy
between you and Him. Let Him have
that one last thing, the last barrier and
film to a life of blessedness; and glory
will come, filling your soul.

(7) What we give, Christ takes; and
at the moment of our giving it. There
may, perhaps, be no rush of emotion.
We may have no inward evidence of

the momentous change in our position.
The reckoning may have for many days
to be one, not of feeling, but of faith.
We can only say, "I am His; because I
gave, and He took." But sooner or
later we become aware that the flames
of the heavenly fire have fallen on our
sacrifice; feeding on it; appropriating
it; cleansing it; and preparing it for
blessed, holy service.

It is very important to realize this
point. In consecration we make the
same mistake, as is so prevalent in conversion; of trying to feel in ourselves
that Christ has taken us. We must believe He takes that which we commit
to Him; though no angel comes to as-
sure us that we are henceforth His own,

What we give, God takes; and He
takes it in fire. We do not always realize
all that is involved. But it is sublime
to tread the glowing embers of that fire,
with the Son of God at our side, knowing that the restraining bonds are shri-

velling at every step, and that not a hair of our head can perish.

This is CONSECRATION. And from this glad hour the surrendered one dares to begin appropriating Christ: a blessed habit, which by the grace of the Holy Spirit becomes the practice of the life. Reader, be persuaded to take this step. Seek some lonely spot, some still hour, and give yourself to Him who gave Himself for you on the Cross; and who waits to give Himself continually to you in response to the claims of your appropriating faith.

III.

Reciprocal Indwelling.

"Abide in Me, and I in you."— *John xv. 4.*

"THAT I may dwell in the house of the Lord all the days of my life" was the aspiration of the man after God's own heart. (Psalm xxvii. 4.) It became his saintly soul, but it cannot be literally realized in these days, when there is no longer a material earthly sanctuary. And yet there is a sense in which that wish may be verified in the history of us all. What is "the house of the Lord," but the conscious presence of the Lord? And they who have acquired the blessed habit of perpetually recollecting the nearness of Jesus know something, at least, of that "dwelling in the secret place of the Most High," and "abiding under the shadow of the Almighty," of which the Psalmist sang. (Psalm xci.)

If only we could acquire that blessed habit, and maintain that hallowed attitude of spirit, we should need few exhortations beside. We should be perfectly satisfied with—Himself. We should hold all things in Him. We should fear no foe, fighting under the Captain's eye. We should be set free from the power of besetting sin, as the fire in our grates is extinguished when the sun shines brilliantly upon the glowing embers. How strong—how sweet—how happy—should we be, if only we could dwell in the unbroken enjoyment of the presence of the King!—so that He should be first in every thought, and act, and moment of life.

You say that this may be possible for the priest, or the saint, but not for those who are harassed with daily care: for

the cloister, but not for the market: for
the holy day, but not for the working
day, with its dust and clamor. Yet,
surely, since the Master bids us all to
abide in Him, and stays not to limit His
meaning, or define the character of
those who are welcome to stand continually in His presence, we must infer
that He wishes to make no distinction,
but to admit all His servants to share in
the bright and blessed privilege.

But can the mind be occupied with
two thoughts at once? Perhaps not:
yet—though it may be impossible for
the mind to entertain at the same instant more than one train of ideas—
beneath the mind there is the heart, with
all its sensibilities and deep emotional
life, instantly and always alive to the
presence or absence of some beloved
object, even when the mind is most
busily engaged.

The orator is conscious of the presence and appreciation of his audience,

even when his intellect is most busily engaged in furnishing the thought which
he is uttering. The business man, absorbed in counting up his books, whilst
his wife is quietly occupied with her work
by his side, is aware of her sweet presence, at the very moment when he is
adding up the longest column of figures.
The young mother may be very busy
about the house, tidying the rooms in
the upper stories, but her heart is always on the alert for the cry of the
babe, whose crib is beside the kitchen
fire. So we may be fully occupied in
thought and act, and yet our heart may
be abiding in holy and blessed communion with our Lord, as "a living
bright reality,

> "More present to Faith's vision keen
> Than any earthly object seen;
> More dear, more intimately nigh
> Than e'en the closest earthly tie."

But before this blessed consciousness
of the presence of Christ can be ours,
we must know experimentally the mean-

ing of the Apostle's words, "Christ liveth in me." (Gal. ii. 20.) In point of
fact, there is a lovely reciprocity in this
indwelling. We abide IN HIM, because
He abides IN US. In the translucent
depths of southern seas, the voyager is
aware of the infinite variety of sponge-
growth, waving to and fro with the gentle
movement of the tide; and the ocean is
in the sponge, whilst the sponge is in
the ocean, illustrating the reciprocal indwelling of the believer in Christ, and
Christ in the believer. Take the common iron poker from your fireside, and
place it amid the fiery bed of burning
coals, and soon it becomes red-hot, because the fire is in it whilst it is in the
fire. Shall the time not come when we
shall learn the secret of a life of ardent
devotion and glowing zeal, because we
have mastered the lesson of the reciprocal indwelling of the saint and the
Saviour?

This was the secret of the human life

of Christ.   He dwelt in his Father's
love, whilst there rang through His
being the glad consciousness that He
did always those things which gave
pleasure to his Father's heart. And the
Father dwelt in Him, manifesting His
Divine presence by words of grace and
works of power.   Have you ever truly
realized that Jesus Christ is literally
within you—the Divine tenant and oc-
cupant of the inner shrine?   Do not feel
obliged to dilute or water down this
wondrous fact, as if it were too marvellous to be accepted in its literal force.
We cannot understand it; we cannot
reason it out with our poor logic; we
cannot account for it; we can only sit
down in amazed wonder and exclaim,
"Wherefore is this come to me, that I
should be a temple for the Lord God of
Hosts?" And when once we can realize
the literal force of "in you," we shall
enter upon the glorious and perpetual
enjoyment of "ye in Me."   The two are

reciprocal: and the measure of our appreciation of the one is the measure of our enjoyment of the other.

There are four texts in the New Testament in which the truth of this reciprocity of indwelling is taught, each time with a specific purpose.

I. As to Fellowship—"He that eateth My flesh, and drinketh My blood, dwelleth in me, and I in Him." (John vi. 56.) Whatever else is meant by that mystic feeding on Christ, this at least is included—that, through the help of the Holy Ghost, we are to set apart daily periods of time for fellowship with the living Saviour. The early morning hour, when we go forth to gather manna, while the day is young; the evening twilight when men go forth to meditate; the hour of solemn worship and gathering with the people of God: all these, and many other golden seasons, are opportunities of nourishing the inner life, with His flesh, which is meat indeed, and His blood, which is drink indeed.

But how often, at such times, the
spirit seems to fail and faint! It cannot
disengage itself from the birdlime of
worldliness which fastens it down.
It cannot shake off the buzzing cloud of
teasing, wandering thoughts. It resem-
bles, as Jeremy Taylor says, a lark trying in vain to rise against a strong east
wind.

What then should be our resource?
We may turn from personal supplication
to intercession on the behalf of others;
or we may open the Word of God, and
begin to study its pages, as men pour
water into a dry pump to make it draw;
or we may appropriate the prayers of
the saints of former days. But there is
a more excellent way. Let us sit quietly down to meditate. Let us remember
that the living Saviour, who ever liveth
to pray, is by the Holy Spirit, literally
within us. He who, in the days of His
flesh, climbed the mountains for fellow-

ship with His Father, while the towns
that bordered on the lake were still
swathed in morning mist, is now dwelling in the heart.   Stand aside, then,
cease your strivings and efforts; and let
Him pour forth in and through you the
mighty torrent of his strong cryings and
ceaseless prayers.

It will not be long before you find
your prayers mounting up with freedom
and conscious power to heaven; and in
a moment, by the reciprocity which we
are now considering, you shall become
aware of the literal presence around
you—as a Divine environment—of Him
who once lit up the lone isle of Patmos
by the irradiation of His manifested
glory.

II. As to Obedience.—"He that
keepeth His commandments, dwelleth
in Him, and He in him." (1 John iii. 24.)
There are three things which must focus
in one point before we can be sure of

the will of God: The prompting of the
Spirit within; the teaching of the Word
without; and the concurrence of Providence around—in the events of daily
life.   We should never take a step unless these three concur.   If they do not
so concur, we may be sure that God's
hour is not yet come, and we must stand
still and see His salvation.

But there are times when we clearly
know the Lord's will, but seem unable
to do it.   Our heart and flesh fail.   We
cower before strong opposition.   The
good we would, we do not: the evil we
would not, we do.

How shall we do then?   Shall we
lash ourselves forward by reproaches
and remonstrances, as the galley-slaves
of old were urged to more frantic ex-
ertions by the strokes of the knout?
Not so!   We are no longer under the
law, but under grace.   God does not
leave us thus to cope with ourselves.
There is another and a better way,

which lies within the text already cited,
if its identical propositions are reversed,
"He that dwelleth in Him, and He in
him, keepeth His commandments."

Remember, again, that the Lord
Jesus is in you as the very power of
God.   During His earthly life He bore
the significant title of "Servant" of God,
who, when the Lord God opened His
ear, was not rebellious nor turned away
back, nor swerved a hair's-breadth from
the narrow path of implicit obedience.
(Psa. xvii. 1–6.)   Why should not He
work in you and through you, as of old
He wrought through His mortal body?
Let Him have the opportunity! Cease
from your own works, as the Son did
from His.   And as He emptied Himself,
so that the Father which dwelt in Him
was really the doer of His works, so
empty yourself of your own efforts and
strivings, and let Him work in you to
will and to do of His own good pleasure.
You will soon be delivered from impo-

tence, and indolence, and failure, and
you will find yourself energized mightily in all manner of strenuous and noble
deeds.

And this will be the result by the law
of reciprocity, which we are elaborating
—that you will become aware of the
literal presence of Him who appeared
to Joshua as the Captain of the Lord's
host.   You will be ready to kneel before
Him in lowly homage, and to await His
commands; and you will carry with you
a consciousness of the fact that you are
ever living in the very midst of the encompassing glory of the King of saints
"In Him we live, and move, and have
our being."   (Acts xvii. 28.)

III.   As to Confession. — "Whosoever shall confess that Jesus is the Son
of God, God dwelleth in him, and He in
God." (1 John iv. 15.)   The days are
past in which every confessor was called
to be a martyr.   And yet confession is

hard enough: it is not easy to stand up
for Christ in the commercial room, or
in the workshop, in the railway carriage,
or amid the frivolities of a drawing-
room. There is a natural proneness in
us all to a false shame, which gags our
mouths, and chokes our utterance, and
keeps us silent, when we know we ought
to speak.

Ah, how bitterly we reproach ourselves then and afterwards; as we see
the opening gradually close, and feel
that the chance for quiet remonstrance,
or for words of entreaty and expostula-
tion, has gone never to return. (Rev.
ii. 13.)

And yet we have failed so often, we
have almost lost heart. Can it ever
be different, we being what we are?
Can we ever resemble Antipas, the faithful confessor? Can we ever be bold as
a lion for Him who has never given us
just cause for shame? Indeed, matters
will never mend until we abandon our

own feeble attempts and draw heavily on the glorious fact of His mighty indwelling. We can do nothing; but all things are possible to Him. Let us only give Him the chance. Let us place ourselves at His disposal to speak in us, and through us, as He will. Let Him have His blessed way with us. Before Pontius Pilate He witnessed a good confession: why may we not expect Him to repeat it, through us, the meanest of the members of His body; who long to be possessed of Him, even as of old men were the mediums through which lost spirits spoke and wrought.

And none can thus abandon themselves to Him without becoming aware, through the law of reciprocal indwelling, that Christ in the heart means the heart in Christ; and that dependence on the indwelling Saviour will invariably induce a vivid consciousness of the indwelling of the human spirit in the light of His gracious presence.

IV. As to Love.—"He that dwelleth in love dwelleth in God, and God in Him." (1 John iv. 16.) We must love people whom we cannot like; with whom we have no natural sympathy; and who seem made to irritate us. It is easy to like nice people. No special grace is required for this. Our affections naturally entwine around the amiable and gentle; and, if these alone filled our homes, there would be no education in the Divine art of loving. We only learn what the love of God is when we have to do with people who defy our own powers of affection. The fairest powers of nature are never so apparent as when they are called in to drape the rents in the earth's surface, or to clothe some unsightly rock, rearing its form amid a paradise of beauty.

Is there such a person in your life, the source of constant chafe, annoyance, fret? You feel you cannot love,

you cannot speak gently, or stroke that
fretful face, or find pleasure in that un-
congenial presence? Anything but that.
You could be lovely if only you were
thrown with a congenial temperament.
Yet how much you would miss of Divine
education! Do this. Fall back on the
memory of the Divine indwelling: and
since the strong Son of God, who is Immortal Love, is in you, let Him love
that loveless one through you; let Him
pour a torrent of love through you, as
the channel and medium of blessing;
let His love speak through your voice,
and look through your eyes, and nerve
your fingers. Love with His love. You
can do all things through Christ that
strengtheneth you.

And, again, let us repeat it. You will
find that you cannot act thus without
bringing into operation that reciprocity
of indwelling which is our theme; and
you will know, as never before, what it
is to have Christ encompassing you be-

hind and before, and covering you with
the warm, safe protection of those
feathers, to which He called Jerusalem.
(Matt. xxiii. 37; Luke xiii. 34.)

What more need we say? The Spirit
can alone reveal the truth we try to
teach. But He will gladly perform this
His appointed office. And thus we
shall come to understand what it is ever
"to dwell in the secret place of the
Most High, and to abide under the
shadow of the Almighty." (Psalm
xci. 7.)

IV.

"Sin" and "Sins."

THE nearer we live to God, the more
sensitive we become to the presence
of sin. Increasing light means increasing self-judgment; and things which
were allowed in the twilight of the
dawn, become abhorrent as the noontide
light reveals their true character. You
may guage your growth in grace, and
your increasing reception of the Holy
Spirit, by the tenderness of your conscience with respect to sins which you
once permitted without remorse, and
almost without remark. In proportion
as you comprehend the full beauty of

Christ your Lord, you will find imperfections in your best moments, and discern blemishes in your holiest deeds. When we *hear* of God, we are self-satisfied; but when we *see* Him, we abhor ourselves, and repent in dust and ashes.

In view of these facts it is impossible for any true child of God to be contented with himself. He cannot speak of himself as having attained, or as being already perfect. He is ever following after to apprehend or attain; and as he does so, he, who once described himself as the least of all saints, comes to call himself the chief of sinners. He is conscious of forgiveness; he knows that he is accepted in the Beloved; but, in proportion as he walks in the growing light, he feels his growing need of the precious blood, which cleanseth from all sin.

It is true that many claim to have attained to a condition of sinless perfectness; but they surely fail to discriminate between things which differ widely as

the poles.   They do not distinguish between the believer's standing in Christ
Jesus, in the sight of God, and the
practical realization and appropriation
of that standing, which can only be in
proportion to his faith.   According to
our faith, so it is to us; and, as faith is
ever growing towards perfect vision, is
it not clear that there must also be a
growth towards the perfect appreciation
and enjoyment of our standing in Christ
Jesus?

And is there not this also, that there
is a whole world of difference between
freedom from conscious sin and the
attainment of the perfect glory of the
stature of Christ?   The one is negative;
the other is positive.   The one is according to the dim light of human consciousness; the other is according to the
Divine standard of infinite excellence.
The one is within the reach of the young
disciple, and ranks among the elements
of Christ; the other is still in advance

of the holiest saint among the ranks of the redeemed, and always will be.

When we come short, we sin.

As soon as we put ourselves in the true relation to the Spirit of God, we may expect to be kept from conscious sin; but surely this is a very different thing from the perfection of the New Testament, which is the maturity of the fully developed man. Even if we have passed from the adolescence to the manhood of Christian development, there is still an infinite chasm between our uttermost attainment, and the surpassing loveliness of the One Perfect Man.

Who of us has not also had some such experience as this—that we condemn things which passed muster years ago? Is not this the law of growing excellence in all art, in all knowledge? Does not the singer, the painter, the writer, the poet, detect blemishes and flaws where once the judgment rested with entire acquiescence and content? And must not

this be always so, as long as there is
progress in any direction along which
the energies of the soul may work? And
if this be so, is it not almost certain that
we permit and harbor things to-day
which we shall be the first to condemn
when years have passed; just as we condemn things to-day which, for want of
fuller light, seemed harmless enough in
the days of our ignorance? But, under
such circumstances, how can we say
that we are perfect? How can we speak
of ourselves as sinless? How can we ever
get beyond the need of humbly confess-
ing that we are sinners? How can we
do without the constant washing in the
laver of priests?

There are three matters which must
be considered in connection with the
believer's inner experience of evil:—

I. THE TEMPTER.

"Your adversary the devil, as a roar-
ing lion, walketh about, seeking whom

he may devour: whom resist." (I Peter v. 8, 9.)

It is not necessary to suppose that the prince of the power of the air is the author of temptation to every believer, the world over; for that would go near to investing him with the attributes of omniscience and omnipresence. But he is surrounded by legions of inferior spirits, the wicked spirits in heavenly places, as malignant in their hate as he is; and who are ever waiting to carry out his plans: and any one of these is sufficient to master the soul that has not learnt the secret of victory through faith in the Stronger than the strong man armed.

It is a commonplace in Christian ethics—and yet it may not be realized by every reader of these lines—that temptation does not become sin to us, until the will assents to the suggestion of the Tempter. So long as the will is resolute, exclaiming with Joseph, "How can I do

this great wickedness, and sin against
God?" there is no sin. Sin is the act
of the perverted will. That temptation
is not sin is proved by the fact that the
Lord Jesus was tempted in all points,
though without sin. Of course, there
is a vast difference between Him and us:
because there was nothing in Him, as
there is in us, responsive to the tempter's
suggestions.   It is difficult for us to
listen to the suggestion of sin without
contracting any stain; but still it may
be accepted as broadly true that the
fact of our being tempted does not
necessarily involve us in sin.

There is only one way by which the
Tempter can be met. He laughs at our
good resolutions and ridicules the
pledges with which we fortify ourselves.
He has been dealing with these for
sixty centuries, and well knows how to
find their weakest point, and to sweep
them away, as the tide does the child's
barricade of sand. There is only One

whom he fears; One who in the hour of
greatest weakness conquered him; and
who has been raised far above all prin-
cipality and power, that He may succor
and deliver all frail and tempted souls.
He conquered the prince of this world
in the days of His flesh; and He is prepared to do as much again, and yet
again, in each one of us, if only we will
truly surrender ourselves to His gracious
and mighty indwelling.

In the days of knightly chivalry it
was supposed to be enough for the true
soldier of the cross to make the sacred
sign upon his person; and instantly the
foul spirits that had gathered in the murky gloom to do him harm, fell back, and
let him through. It was not all legend
and myth. But there is a truth beneath
the mediæval setting. And that truth is
ours to-day—that the best resource for
the hardly-beset soldier of Jesus is to
appeal, not to the cross, but to Him
who on that cross bruised the serpent's

head, not for Himself only, but for us.

There are many forms in which that appeal may be made. Some utter the name of the tempted—the succoring—High Priest: "Jesus! Jesus!" Some cry in the triumphant assurance of victory, "Jesus saves me." Some do better still, and claim that grace in Him, the lack of which is hurrying them into sin; so that temptation becomes a positive means of grace to them, by showing their deficiency, and leading them to strengthen the things which remain, but which may be languishing to death.

But whichever method you adopt, reader, be sure you do it in one way or another. Swift as the chick to the shelter of the mother's wing, so do you betake yourself to the ever-offered protection of Jesus Christ whenever menaced by the Tempter. The Lord God is not only a sun but a shield. "The name of the Lord is a strong tower: the righteous runneth into it and is safe.

He will "cover thy head in the day of battle." (Ps. lxxxiv. 11; Prov. xviii. 10; Ps. cxl. 7.)

It may be that you have tried to do this, and have failed. You have entered upon the day's life, fully intending to make Jesus your shield of faith, and to hide in Him when threatened by the Tempter. Yet you have found to your dismay, that you have been overcome before you have bethought yourself of your refuge and deliverer. But there is an easy remedy for this, in the aid of the Holy Spirit. He is the Divine remembrancer. It is his office to maintain the spirit in a state of holy recollectedness; and, if the attack be as a thunderclap, He will be as the premonitory lightning flash, crying, "Beware! Beware! 'turn you to your stronghold, O prisoner of hope.'" (Zech. x. 12.)

Be sure of this, that Satan cannot tempt you beyond what you have power to sustain or resist. Powerless in your-

self, you can do all things in Christ that
strengtheneth you. The Lord Jesus
hath bought you; and you must *trust*
Him to keep you. "The Lord is thy
keeper." "He will not suffer thy foot
to be moved." "Surely He shall deliver
thee from the snare of the fowler." (Ps.
cxxi. 5, 3; xci. 3.)

II. The Sinful Tendency Within.

Regeneration is not the eradication o.
the principle of the old life, but the in
sertion beside it of the principle of a new
life—the Christ life. And these two
exist side by side; as the house of
Saul and the house of David in the
rent and distracted kingdom of Israel:
but the one is destined to get weaker
and weaker, whilst the other waxes
stronger and stronger.

"That which is born of the flesh is
flesh," and can never be anything else
than flesh. It can never be improved
into spirit. It can never be anything

but abhorrent in the eye of the Holy
God. So that "they that are in the flesh
cannot please God"; and the flesh
which is in us can never please God. The
only thing to be done is to deny it; and
to reckon it as a dead thing, which has
no place in the Home of Life. "Bury
thy dead out of thy sight."

SELF is the anagram of FLESH. The
flesh-principle is the self-principle,
which so insidiously creeps into everything from which it is not rigorously
excluded by the grace of God. Before
we are converted self is the sole motive-
power of our lives: our kindest and best
actions originate in this root. And after
we are converted, it strives to insinuate
itself into our religious life. Satan will
not prohibit us from being religious—if
only "self" is the mainspring of our devotion. Hence it is that Jesus Christ is
so unrelenting in His demand for self-
denial. And it has been the axiom of
saintship in all ages—"Wheresoever

thou findest thyself, deny thyself."
Sword in hand, we must pursue this
evil thing—this self-hood—through all
the disguises beneath which it hides
itself.   We must allow it no quarter.
We must believe that it is never more
near or more dangerous than when it
causes a rumor to be set on foot that it
is no more.   In the self-congratulation
which arises on the receipt of this happy
intelligence, there is a new and striking
evidence of its continued and vigorous
existence.

It is to this evil principle, which is
very susceptible to the least suggestion
from without, that the Tempter appeals.
His attacks would be less formidable if
it were not for this traitor within the
citadel of the soul.   But, we may well
fear the bombshells thrown in from
without, when we remember the maga-
zines of gunpowder within, awaiting the
spark that shall hurry them into explo-
sion, and shatter the rest of the soul.

There is no evidence, then, that the flesh shall ever be eradicated, because it is OURSELVES; and the Apostle clearly tells us that "the flesh lusteth against the Spirit, and the Spirit against the flesh." And in those who most earnestly asseverate its eradication in their own experience, there are frequent indications of its presence still. (Gal. v. 17.)

But THIS is possible. The Holy Spirit is the deadly antagonist of, and all-sufficient antidote to, the self-life. When He dwells in blessed fulness within the surrendered heart, He sets it free from the law of sin and death: He annihilates the power of the self-life; as an antiseptic cancels the death-dealing germs which proceed from the body of a patient who is stricken by an infectious disease.

When the Holy Spirit resides in power in the heart, He keeps the self-life so utterly in the place of death that temptation has no fascination, no power. The

appeals of hell are flung against the ear
of death: there is no response, no mo-
tion of obedience. Try it, reader: be
not content to have the Holy Spirit
within thee; see that He fills thee; and
thou wilt experience that blessed condition in which the sparks of temptation shall seem to be quenched in an
ocean of water, as they touch thy heart.

But remember the evil thing is there
still; not eradicated, not destroyed, only
kept in the place of death by the Spirit
of life. And if ever thou shalt quench
or limit His gracious operation, so that
He relaxes His restraining power, that
accursed principle will arise with all its
pristine force, join hands with the
tempter, and hurry thee into sin. Watch
and pray, therefore; keep in with the
Holy Ghost; walk warily; that thou
mayest never have to retrace thy steps,
shedding tears of blood.

III. SINS.

Through neglect of watching and prayer — or by reason of carelessness in the walk and conversation — it is quite possible to break that holy connection between ourselves and heaven which is the secret of deliverance, and the talisman of victory. There is always a Delilah ready to shear off the locks of our strength, if we allow ourselves to sleep in her lap. And our strength may be gone ere we know it. "He wist not that the Lord had departed from him." (Jud. xvi. 20.)

And when we put ourselves outside those sacred influences which are intended to deliver us from the power of evil, there is no alternative but that we should break out again into acts of sin. But there is a difference. They are not now the normal state of the soul. They are committed in opposition to the judgment and the conscience. They are the sins of a child for which it will

be chastened, until it gets back into the
old blessedness again. An old divine
says: "A sheep and a sow may each
fall into the same quagmire; but the
sow will wallow in it, whilst the sheep
will bleat piteously, until she is extri-
cated and cleansed." Such is the difference between the ungodly and the
children of God. "Whosoever abideth
in Him sinneth not"; that is, sin can
never become his normal and habitual
state. (1 John iii. 6.)

If ever this should be your unhappy
lot, do not despair. The true test of
Christian character does not consist in
the inability to fall, but in the quick
agony of repentance, and in the im-
mediate restoration to the ways which
had been left. Directly you are conscious of sin, turn at once to your com-
passionate Lord. Do not wait for the
fever of passion to subside, or for the
agony of your shame to die down; but,
there and then, in the crowd or the

street, lift up your heart, and ask Him to touch you with that finger before which uncleanness cannot abide: ask Him to wash you as he did the feet of His disciples, soiled by jealousy and strife for mastery: ask Him to restore your soul to the place it occupied before you fell.

You may not be able to forgive yourself: but He will forgive you instantly; the stain will be at once extracted from the spirit's robes; the foulness will immediately flee from the blemished dress; and the forgiven one shall occupy again the place which for a moment had been vacated, the place in the heavenlies, side by side with its Redeemer. Oh, do not doubt the Saviour's willingness, or the Saviour's power, to forgive; or the efficacy of His blood to wash out each stain, as it may become manifest to the quickened conscience. Remember that His blood ever cleanseth from all sin, as the stream is ever flowing over the pebble, and as the tear-water is ever removing from the eye the motes that alight for a moment upon its surface.

It is not an easy world for any of us to traverse; it is no friend to grace: but it is possible to walk through it with clean and stainless robes. Sin may assail; but it will be as the waves that beat outside the goodly ship without finding admittance within its walls. And out of the pure and guileless heart shall spring all the loveliness of unselfish and helpful deeds, such as shall make this sad world happier, and dark hearts bright with the light of heaven.

O souls, weary and sin-sick, hand yourselves over to the tender mercies of the Good Physician, sure that He will undertake the most desperate case; and "give beauty for ashes, the oil of joy for mourning, the garment of praise for the spirit of heaviness." (Isaiah lxi. 3.)

V.

The Will.

"If ye be willing and obedient, ye shall eat the good of the land." —*Isaiah i. 19.*

"Thy people shall be willing in the day of Thy power." —*Psalm cx. 3.*

THE one question which the Lord Jesus puts to every one of us, is that which He put, beside Bethesda's pool, to the sufferer who wistfully scanned His face for help: "*Wilt* thou be made whole?" The whole question turns on the attitude of the will. And it is for lack of realizing this, that many grope for years in darkness, who might otherwise walk in the light of life.

There are some who lay the chief stress on *Right Thinking*. They demand that the mind should have a clear ap-

prehension of the entire system of
Christian truth.   Every *i* must have its
dot; every *t* must be strictly crossed.
Each doctrine must receive its just place
in the homage of the soul; and there
must be no uncertainty in the pronun-
ciation of the test-words of the Church.
Then, they argue, that the character and
experience will necessarily be right and
blessed.

But, in practice, it is not so.   It is impossible to exaggerate the importance
of clear and accurate conceptions of
truth.   For what a man believes, that
he is.   At the same time, experience
and observation prove beyond a doubt,
that to think right is not enough to produce the fruits of the Spirit, or the
blessedness of the Beatitudes.   Many
babes and sucklings in knowledge, whose
notions of truth, through no fault of
their own, are hazy and partial, have
entered the kingdom of heaven; the
doors of which are closed against the

wise and prudent who have no other claim for entrance than that they could pass muster in the strictest theological examination.

Others lay the chief stress on *Right Feeling*. Their test of rightness is joyousness. When they feel bright and happy, and their heart sings—and the azure blue, unflecked by cloud, canopies their path—they can sit in the heavenlies, and take their place among their peers. But when their glad emotions expend themselves as summer brooks; and the birds cease their strains; and the sky is overcast; they begin to question even their acceptance.

Surely feeling is too unsatisfactory for any of us to build upon it for peace or power. Choose rather the shifting quicksands as a foundation for your house! We need something more reliable than an experience—which may be disturbed by an east wind, a cloudy day, or a fit of indigestion.

The true basis of religion is in *Right-willing*. And the reason for this is clear. We are not what we know. We are not what, in some special moment, we feel. We are what we will. We must bore down beneath the alluvial deposits of emotion, and the formation of the intellect, to the granite of the will! There, and there only, can we find a stable basis on which to build the structure of a blessed or useful life; because the will is the true expression of ourselves.

We admit this in daily life. We judge men, not by their intellectual capacity, not by the sensibilities that quiver beneath the passing breath, as the chords of an Æolian lyre; not by exceptional and special deeds: but by their WILL — which may be called the resolve and intention of the soul, expressing itself in the decisions and actions of the life.

We do not blame the maniac who seeks to fire a cathedral: we simply confine him; his will was impaired. But we condemn the man who clearly meant to take his brother's life, though the deed itself was frustrated; his will was murder. And what we are with respect to one another, that we are also with respect to the Almighty God. His one complaint against us is not that we are dull and stupid; or that we do not feel more deeply; or that we are not swifter and stronger in our obedience—but that we are *not, willing.* "Ye *will not* come unto Me, that ye might have life." "If any man *will* come after Me." "I would....but ye *would not.*" "If ye be *willing* and obedient, ye shall eat the good of the land."

We need not now touch that mysterious province, hidden from mortal ken, where the human will is influenced by the Divine will. Doubtless, there are avenues by which the will of God reaches us, and touches us, of which we know nothing. And there are numberless methods by which God's will can impress itself on ours without violating the individuality of our willinghood. It is enough to know that He does work in us to *will* and to do of His own good pleasure. And it is certain that we cannot will aright except He prompt us. More than this we do not know, and cannot say. We cannot but think, however, that no soul of man is born outside the range of the working of that loving will, which is peace on earth and good will to men. Alas, that it is so often resisted, even unto death!

Now let us turn to the practical bearing of this great truth—that our primary concern must ever be with our WILL. And we may sum up all we have to say in this one sentence: Put your will on God's side in everything, and leave to Him the responsibility of fulfilling in you, and through you, "all the good pleasure of His goodness, and the work of faith with power; that the name of our Lord Jesus Christ may be glorified in you, and ye in Him, according to the grace of our God, and the Lord Jesus Christ." (2 Thess. i. 11, 12.)

ON THE THRESHOLD OF SALVATION.

How many there are around us like the impotent man of Bethesda! They are waiting for healing with eager desire. To get it they linger for years in the porches of Mercy's House. They wistfully see the gladness with which many go healed away. They hope that their turn will come at last.

But they are waiting for the wrong thing—for some mysterious troubling of the waters, rather than for the Healer. For a ceremony, and not for Christ. For an angel, and not for the Saviour. For the help of men to put them into salvation, or to their own lame efforts to shuffle into the pool of healing. They are always trying to get more correct conceptions of Christianity, or to work themselves up into a condition of earnest feeling. Oh, if they could only *feel* more earnestness; or more adequate sorrow for sin; or more assurance of faith! They wait year after year for some angel to trouble the inner waters of their souls, and send a ripple of saving feeling across them. But the angel comes not. And they wait on till hope almost dies.

To such the Saviour comes. "*Wilt* thou be made whole?" He does not send the soul to college to study a creed, however Apostolic. He does not wait till it is fired with ardor or steeped in tears. He cuts right through all sorrowful confessions of deficient faith, utter worthlessness, inability to shed pure tears or think right thoughts. All this is with Him secondary. It must be considered: but presently, not first. His one prime concern is the will. What *willest* thou? *Wilt* thou be saved? The question of salvation is a moral one; it hinges on the will.

And if the trembling soul can only look up to Him and say; "I would, but I cannot, feel; I would, but I cannot, believe; I would, but I cannot, repent"; then with great joy the Shepherd takes the lost sheep upon His shoulders. He says: "It is enough. I will work in thee all thou lackest. I will enter through the unlatched door of thine heart, laden with gifts. I will cleanse thee from all that grieves Me; and I will produce in thee all those holy things which thou seekest. They are the gifts of God to the recipient spirit through the agency of the Holy Spirit."

The initial step of salvation is our willingness to be saved. If that is assured, tell Christ so. Look to Him to begin in thee His gracious work. And there is already commenced in thee a transformation, which starts with forgiveness, and ends in perfect conformity to the Son of God, in heaven's dateless glory.

IN OUR DAILY RELIGIOUS EXPERIENCE.

We give ourselves to God. Beneath the spell of some stirring appeal, or under the impression of written words, burning as the carbon-points of the electric light, we resolve that we will live a more earnest, devoted, and whole-hearted existence. For some few days the momentum carries us on, and we feel happy and satisfied.

But after awhile the blessing we have received seems to expend itself. We are troubled by violent temptation. We lose all pleasure in private prayer. We can get nothing from our Bibles. For some deep and subtle reason, all our feelings are suddenly overcast. The heart, which was like a garden in summer, is as a barren moor, on which clouds brood. At such a time, if we are simply dependent on our feelings, we shall be ready to despair. If, like Peter, we regard the winds and waves, we, like him, must begin to sink; and we shall doubt the reality of the experience of God's truth and grace, which had given us a real lift heavenwards.

But if, my reader, you have ever learnt the side of truth on which we are laying stress, you will have an unbroken confidence, and will feel a handrail ready to your touch, though you cannot see your way through the murky night. At such a time look up to Christ and say: "I do not feel as I did; the joy of song and rapture, all is gone: but I am still Thine; I will to be only, always, all for Thee; I desire, in the very centre and heart of my being, to abide in Thee; I long for nothing so much as that Thou shouldest hasten Thy work of conquest within my soul, till every thought and feeling are brought captive to Thine obedience."

Even if you are conscious of having swerved for a moment from the path of perfect willinghood, by His grace put your WILL back again on the side of

Christ, with tears and confessions, and ask Him to hold it, as a father holds the hand of his child on a slippery day. Forget your feelings. Entrench yourself in your WILL. Ask Jesus to purify and sanctify it by His Spirit, so that it may be true to Himself. And believe that He is as eager as you are to still all the rebellion of the soul, and to make you what you wish and WILL to be, in your best and holiest hours. Your attitude towards Christ is determined, not by your feelings, but by your steadfast desire and "will."

In Sorrow and Trial.

As sons we must endure the rod of chastening, which is "not joyous but grievous." The way to the Kingdom lies through Gethsemane, with its deep shadows and its tears, and sweat of blood. All that can abide the fire must be made to pass through the fire.

And when our hour comes we cannot but suffer. We suffer as the little one is torn from our embrace, not realizing henceforth there will be always a child in our home. We suffer, as we have to leave cherished surroundings, and venture, as the eagle's nestlings, on the untried air. We suffer, as we have to be the means of inflicting pain upon those who love us; at the call of God taking the knife to slay their hopes. We suffer as we see some creeping paralysis slowly cut us off from the avenues of sense and life; shutting us up in a living cell. And let us not begrudge it all, since we learn obedience by the things we suffer; and discover the art of comforting others as we have been comforted.

Yet sometimes how hard it is to be submissive! And here it is that so many mistake. They try to *feel* submissive and resigned. But they try in vain. They cannot bring themselves to feel, as they know they ought: and so they write hard things against themselves; and go out into the night in a self-imposed exile.

But it would be comparatively easy if they would only begin with the WILL. Will God's will. Tell Him that you are willing to be made willing to have His will. Bring your will to Him, as a piece of cold iron; and ask Him to renew it, and soften it, and mould it into perfect oneness with His own. Say to Him as Jesus did, "Father, Thy will, not mine, be done!" And when thoughts of rebellion or mistrust surge upwards in your soul, do not lose heart; trust God to deal with them. You cannot master them; but God can. Only be sure that your will is true to Him as the needle is to the pole.

Oh, is not this a sight on which angels love to dwell?—when a human soul, amid its keenest agony, still is able to will the will of God; not swerving from it to the right or to the left; sure it must be good and wise, though all appearances are contrary; and daring to cry out from the midst of its agony, whilst all the nature beside is in revolt, "My God, I trust Thee; I choose Thy will."

If thus we yield our will to God, in our blindness, not because we feel it pleasant, but because we dare to believe in Him, we shall find that a wonderful change will steal over us, winning over our emotions and feelings to the self-same side; so that we shall come to accept the will of God with our feelings, as well as to will it with our will.

In Regard to Sin.

When temptation besets us, it will sometimes so insinuate itself into our hearts, that we may be at a loss to distinguish the voice of the tempter from that of our own consciousness.

Bunyan tells us, that when the pilgrim was come over against the mouth of the pit, one of the wicked ones got behind him and whisperingly suggested many grievous blasphemies to him, which he verily thought had proceeded from his own mind. This put poor Christian more to it than anything that he had met with before.

We all of us know something of this. Such horrid thoughts! Such vain imaginations! Such vile suggestions! Noisome pestilence, indeed! But it is not ours so long as the will remains steadfast in the grace that is in Christ Jesus. Nor can we be held chargeable of sin so long as the spirit cleaves its way through all, tossing the suggestions aside as a ship the foam-crested waves.

Will to be free! *Will* to walk with God in stainless robes! *Will* to refuse the tempting bait! *Will* to deny flesh and to crucify self! *Will* because God is working in you to will. And you will find that if the WILL is present with you, the power to perform will also be forthcoming to your faith; and Jesus will make haste to achieve your complete deliverance. Lift up your heads and rejoice: your redemption draweth near.

Yes, and this will come to you—that your will shall become more and more one with the will of God: so much so, that God will give you the keys of His kingdom, saying, "Ask what ye *will*, and it shall be done unto you." And in proportion as the will of man is brought into unison and harmony with the will of God, there will be growing peace and growing power. When the will of God is done in the heart, even as it is done in heaven, then the joy of heaven enters it to abide. "Eye hath not seen, nor ear heard, nor hath the heart of man conceived, what God hath prepared for them that love Him." But these things are unfolded to the man who has given up his will to God; and who has received it back again, magnetized by His will; and who now lives in the citidel of a sanctified and devoted will. For this is the law of the kingdom of the Son of

God: "If any man wills to do His will, he shall know."

Wilt thou be made whole? Christ asks that question of thee, my reader. Is not the Holy Spirit producing in thee a holy willingness? If so, tell thy Saviour so. He wills; *wilt* thou? If thou dost, then He undertakes to do all the rest; producing in thee health and life, wholeness and everlasting joy.

VI.

Guidance.

"I will guide thee with Mine Eye."—*Psalm xxxii. 8.*

MANY children of God are so deeply exercised on the matter of guidance that it may be helpful to give a few suggestions as to knowing the way in which our Father would have us walk, and the work He would have us do. The importance of the subject cannot be exaggerated; so much of our power and peace consist in knowing where God would have us be, and in being just there.

The manna only falls where the cloudy pillar broods; but it is certain to be found on the sands, which a few hours ago were glistening in the flashing light of the heavenly fire, and are now shadowed by the fleecy canopy of cloud. If

we are precisely where our heavenly
Father would have us to be, we are perfectly sure that He will provide food and
raiment, and everything beside. When
He sends His servants to Cherith, He
will make even the ravens to bring
them food.

How much of our Christian work has
been abortive, because we have persisted
in initiating it for ourselves instead of
ascertaining what God was doing, and
where He required our presence. We
dream bright dreams of success. We
try and command it. We call to our aid
all kinds of expedients, questionable or
otherwise. And at last we turn back, dis-
heartened and ashamed, like children
who are torn and scratched by the bram-
bles, and soiled by the quagmire. None
of this had come about, if only we had
been, from the first, under God's unerring guidance. He might test us, but
He could not allow us to mistake.

Naturally, the child of God, longing

to know his Father's will, turns to the
sacred Book, and refreshes his confidence by noticing how in all ages God
has guided those who dared to trust Him
up to the very hilt; but who, at the time,
must have been as perplexed as we are
often now. We know how Abraham
left kindred and country, and started,
with no other guide than God, across the
trackless desert, to a land which he knew
not. We know how for forty years the
Israelites were led through the peninsula
of Sinai, with its labyrinths of red sand-
stone, and its wastes of sand. We know
how Joshua, in entering the Land of Promise, was able to cope with the difficulties
of an unknown region, and to overcome
great and warlike nations, because he
looked to the Captain of the Lord's Host,
who ever leads to victory. We know
how, in the early Church, the Apostles
were enabled to thread their way through
the most difficult questions, and to solve
the most perplexing problems: laying

down principles which guide the Church
to the end of time; and this because it
was revealed to them as to what they
should do and say, by the Holy Spirit.

*The promises for guidance are unmistak-
able.*

Psa. xxxii. 8: "I will instruct thee and
teach thee in the way which thou shalt
go." This is God's distinct assurance to
those whose transgressions are forgiven,
and whose sins are covered, and who are
more quick to notice the least symptom of His will, than horse or mule to
feel the bit.

Prov. iii. 6: "In all thy ways acknowledge Him, and He shall direct (or make
plain) thy paths." A sure word, on
which we may rest; if only we fulfil the
previous conditions, of trusting with all
our heart, and of not leaning to our own
understanding.

Isa. lviii. 11: "The Lord shall guide
thee continually." It is impossible to
think that He could guide us at all, if

He did not guide us always. For the greatest events of life, like the huge rocking-stones in the West of England, revolve on the smallest points. A pebble may alter the flow of a stream. The growth of a grain of mustard seed may determine the rainfall of a continent. Thus we are bidden look for a Guidance which shall embrace the whole of life in all its myriad necessities.

John viii. 12: "I am the light of the world; he that followeth Me shall not walk in darkness, but shall have the light of life." The reference here seems to be to the wilderness wanderings; and the Master promises to be to all faithful souls, in their pilgrimage to the City of God, all that the cloudy pillar was to the children of Israel on their march to the Land of Promise.

These are but specimens. The vault of Scripture is inlaid with thousands such, that glisten in their measure, as the stars which guide the wanderer across

the deep. Well may the prophet sum up
the heritage of the servants of the Lord,
by saying of the Holy City, "All thy
children shall be taught of the Lord, and
great shall be the peace of thy children."

And yet it may seem to some tried and
timid hearts, as if every one mentioned
in the Word of God was helped, but they
are left without help. They seem to
have stood before perplexing problems,
face to face with life's mysteries, eagerly
longing to know what to do—but no
angel has come to tell them, and no iron
gate has opened to them in the prison-
house of circumstances.

Some lay the blame on their own stu-
pidity. Their minds are blunt and dull.
They cannot catch God's meaning, which
would be clear to others. They are so
nervous of doing wrong, that they cannot learn clearly what is right. "Who
is blind, but My servant? or deaf, as my
messenger that I sent? Who is blind as
he that is perfect, and blind as the Lord's

servant?" Yet, how do we treat our children? One child is so bright-witted and so keen that a little hint is enough to indicate the way; another was born dull; it cannot take in your meaning quickly. Do you only let the clever one know what you want? Will you not take the other upon your knee and make clear to it the directions which baffle it? Does not the distress of the tiny nursling, who longs to know that it may immediately obey, weave an almost stronger bond than that which binds you to the rest? O weary, perplexed, and stupid children, believe in the great love of God, and cast yourselves upon it, sure that He will come down to your ignorance, and suit Himself to your needs, and will take "the lambs in His arms, and carry them in His bosom, and *gently lead* those that are with young."

There are certain practical directions which we must attend to in order that we may be led into the mind of the Lord.

I. OUR MOTIVES MUST BE PURE.

"When thine eye is single, thy whole body also is full of light" (Luke xi. 34). You have been much in darkness lately; and perhaps this passage will point the reason. Your eye has not been single. There has been some obliquity of vision. A spiritual squint. And this has hindered you from discerning indications of God's will, which otherwise had been as clear as noonday.

We must be very careful in judging our motives: searching them as the detectives at the doors of the House of Commons search each stranger who enters. When, by the grace of God, we have been delivered from grosser forms of sin, we are still liable to the subtle working of self, in our holiest and loveliest hours. It poisons our motive. It breathes decay on our fairest fruit-bearing. It whispers seductive flatteries into our pleased ears. It turns the spirit from its holy purpose, as the masses of iron on ocean steamers deflect the needle of the compass from the pole.

So long as there is some thought of personal advantage, some idea of acquiring the praise and commendation of men, some aim at self-aggrandisement, it will be simply impossible to find out God's purpose concerning us. The door must be resolutely shut against all this, if we would hear the still small voice. All cross-lights must be excluded, if we would see the Urim and Thummim stone brighten with God's "Yes," or darken with His "No."

Ask the Holy Spirit to give you the single eye, and to inspire in your heart one aim alone; that which animated our Lord, and enabled Him to cry, as He reviewed His life, "I have glorified Thee on the earth." Let this be the watchword of our lives, "Glory to God in the highest." Then our "whole body shall be full of light, having no part dark, as when the bright shining of a candle doth give light."

II. Our Will Must be Surrendered.

"My judgment is just; because I seek not Mine own will, but the will of the Father which hath sent Me" (John v. 30). This was the secret, which Jesus not only practised, but taught. In one form or another He was constantly insisting on a surrendered will as the key to perfect knowledge, "If any man will do His will, he shall know."

There is all the difference between a will which is extinguished and one which is surrendered. God does not demand that our wills should be withered up like the sinews of a fakir's unused arm. He only asks that they should say "Yes" to Him. Pliant to Him, as the willow twig to the practised hand.

Many a time, as the steamer has neared the quay, have I watched the little lad take his place beneath the poop, with eye and ear fixed on the captain, and waiting to shout each word he utters to the grimy engineers below; and often

have I longed that my will should repeat as accurately and as promptly, the
words and will of God, that all the lower
nature might obey.

It is for lack of this subordination
that we so often miss the guidance we
seek.   There is a secret controversy between our will and God's. And we shall
never be right till we have let Him take,
and break, and make.   Oh, do seek for
that! Never rest till that attitude be
yours.   Hand yourself over to Him to
work in you to will and to do of His own
good pleasure. We must be as plastic
clay, ready to take any shape that the
great Potter may choose: so shall we be
able to detect His guidance.

III.   WE MUST SEEK INFORMATION FOR
        OUR MIND.

This is certainly the next step.   God
has given us these wonderful faculties
of brain power, and He will not ignore
them.   In the days of the Reformation,

He did not destroy the Roman Catholic churches or pulpits; He did better— He preached in them. And in grace, He does not cancel the action of any of His marvellous bestowments; but He uses them for the communication of His purposes and thoughts.

It is of the greatest importance then that we should feed our minds with facts; with reliable information; with the results of human experience; and above all with the teachings of the Word of God. It is matter for the utmost admiration to notice how full the Bible is of biography and history: so that there is hardly a single crisis in our lives that may not be matched from these wondrous pages. There is no book like the Bible for casting a light on the dark landings of human life.

We have no need or right to run hither and thither to ask our friends what we ought to do; but there is no harm in our taking pains to gather all reliable information, on which the flame of holy thought, and consecrated purpose, may feed, and grow strong.   It is for us ultimately to decide as God shall teach us; but His voice may come to us through the voice of sanctified common-sense, acting on the materials we have collected.   Of course, at times God may bid us act against our reason; but these are very exceptional: and then our duty will be so clear that there can be no mistake.   But for the most part, God will speak in the results of deliberate consideration, weighing and balancing the *pros* and *cons*.

When Peter was shut up in prison, and could not possibly extricate himself, an angel was sent to do for him what he could not do for himself; but when they had passed through a street or two of the city, the angel left him to consider the matter for himself.   Thus God treats us still.   He will dictate a miraculous course by miraculous methods.

But when the ordinary light of reason is adequate to the task, He will leave us to act as occasion may serve.

IV. We must be much in Prayer for Guidance.

The Psalms are full of earnest pleadings for clear direction: "Teach me Thy way, O Lord; lead me in a plain path, because of mine enemies." It is the law of our Father's house, that His children shall ask for what they want. "If any of you lack wisdom, let him ask of God, who giveth to all men liberally, and upbraideth not."

In a time of change and crisis, we need to be much in prayer, not only on our knees, but in that sweet form of inward prayer, in which the spirit is constantly offering itself up to God, asking to be shown His will; soliciting that it may be impressed upon its surface, as the heavenly bodies photograph themselves on prepared paper. Wrapt in prayer like this, the trustful believer may tread the deck of the ocean steamer night after night, sure that He who points the stars their courses will not fail to direct the soul which has no other aim than to do His will.

One good form of prayer at such a juncture is to ask that doors may be shut, that the way may be closed, and that all enterprises which are not according to God's will may be arrested at their very beginning, Put the matter absolutely into God's hands from the outset, and He will not fail to shatter the project; and defeat the aim, which is not according to His holy will.

V. WE MUST WAIT THE GRADUAL UNFOLD-ING OF GOD'S PLAN IN PROVIDENCE.

God's impressions within, and His word without, are always corroborated by His providence around; and we should quietly wait until these three focus into one point.

Sometimes it looks as if we are bound to act. Everyone says we must do something; and indeed things seem to have reached so desperate a pitch that we must. Behind are the Egyptians; right and left are inaccessible precipices: before is the sea. It is not easy at such times to stand still and see the salvation of God; but we must. When Saul compelled himself, and offered sacrifice, because he thought that Samuel was too late in coming, he made one of the greatest mistakes of his life.

God may delay to come in the guise of His providence. There was delay ere Sennacherib's host lay like withered leaves around the Holy City. There was delay ere Jesus came walking on the sea in the early dawn, or hastened to raise Lazarus. There was delay ere the angel sped to Peter's side on the night before his expected martyrdom. He stays long enough to test patience of faith, but not a moment behind the extreme hour of need. "The vision is yet for an appointed time, but at the end it shall

speak, and shall not lie; though it tarry,
wait for it: because it will surely come;
it will not tarry."

It is very remarkable how God guides
us by circumstances. At one moment
the way may seem utterly blocked; and
then shortly afterwards some trivial incident occurs, which might not seem
much to others, but which to the keen
eye of faith speaks volumes. Sometimes
these signs are repeated in different
ways, in answer to prayer. They are not
hap-hazard results of chance; but the
opening up of circumstances in the direction in which we should walk. And
they begin to multiply as we advance
towards our goal; just as lights do as we
near a populous town, when darting
through the land by night express.

Sometimes men sigh for an angel to
come to point them their way: that simply indicates that as yet the time has not
come for them to move. If you do not
know what you ought to do, stand still

until you do. And when the time comes
for action, circumstances will sparkle,
like glow-worms, along your path; and
you will become so sure that you are
right, when God's three witnesses concur, that you could not be surer though
and angel-hand beckoned you on.

The circumstances of our daily life are
to us an infallible indication of God's
will, when they concur with the inward
promptings of the Spirit, and with the
Word of God. So long as they are sta-
tionary, wait! When you must act, they
will open; and a way will be made
through oceans and rivers, wastes and
rocks.

We often make a great mistake, thinking that God is not guiding us at all, because we cannot see far ahead. But this
is not His method. He only undertakes
that *the steps* of a good man should be
ordered by the Lord. Not next year;
but to-morrow. Not the next mile; but
the next yard. Not the whole pattern;

but the next stitch in the canvas. If you expect more than this you will be disappointed, and get back into the dark. But this will secure for you leading in the right way; as you will acknowledge when you review it from the hill-tops of glory.

We cannot ponder too deeply the lessons of the cloud given in the exquisite picture-lesson on Guidance in Numbers ix. 15–23. Let us look high enough for guidance. Let us encourage our soul to wait only upon God, till it is given. Let us cultivate that meekness which He will guide in judgment. Let us seek to be of quick understanding, that we may be apt to see the least sign of His will. Let us stand with girded loins and lighted lamps, that we may be prompt to obey. Blessed are those servants! They shall be led by a right way to the golden city of the saints.

VII.

The Fulness of the Spirit.

"Be filled with the Spirit."—*Ephesians v. 18.*

NOTHING can compensate the Church, or the individual Christian, for the lack of the Holy Spirit. What the full stream is to the mill-wheel, that is the Holy Spirit to the Church, What the principle of life is to the body, that is the Holy Spirit to the individual. We shall stand powerless and abashed in the presence of our difficulties and our foes, until we learn what He can be, as a mighty tide of love and power in the hearts of His saints.

Amongst the readers of these lines there may be many who are suffering from different forms of spiritual weakness, all of which are directly attributable to the lack of the Holy Spirit. Not that they are completely destitute of

Him; for if they were, they would not
be Christians at all; but that, being within them, He is present only as an atten-
uated thread, a silver streak, a shallow
brook. Why should we be content with
this? The Pentecostal fulness, the en-
duement of power, the baptism of fire,
are all within our reach. Let us be inspired with a holy ambition to get all that
our God is willing and eager to bestow.

Do you lack *assurance?* Sometimes
you do not, for you feel happy and content. But, anon, these happy hours are
fled, and your rest is broken, as the surface of the mountain tarn is overcast and
ruffled by the gathering storm. You need
a basis of settled peace; and it is only
to be found — first, in a clear apprehen-
sion of what Jesus has done for you;
secondly, in the sealing of the Holy
Spirit. It is His sacred office to witness
with our spirit that we are the children
of God. He is the Spirit of adoption,
whereby we cry, Abba Father!

Do you lack *victory over sin?* This is not to be wondered at, if you neglect the Holy Spirit. He is the blessed antidote to the risings and dominion of the flesh. He lusts against the flesh, so that we may not fulfil its lusts. When He fills the heart in His glorious fulness, the suggestions of temptation are instantly quenched, as sparks in the ocean wave. Sin can no more stand against the presence of the Holy Ghost than darkness can resist the gentle, all-pervasive beams of morning light.

If however He is grieved, or resisted, or quenched, so that His power and presence are restrained, there is no deliverance for the spirit—however bitter its remorse, or eager its resort to fastings, mortifications, and regrets. The law of the Spirit of Life, which is in Christ Jesus, can alone make us free from the law of sin and death. But it can, and it will—if only we yield ourselves to its operation.

Do you lack the *fruits of holiness?* Some whom we know are so evidently filled with the fruits of righteousness, which are to the praise of God, that we are instinctively drawn to them. Their faces are bright with the presence of the Lord, though they drink of the cup of His sorrows. Their spirit is tender; their disposition sweet and unselfish; and their childlike humility flings the halo of indescribable beauty over their whole behaviour.

We lack these graces. There is little in us to attract men to Christ; much to repel. Our boughs are naked and bare as if locusts had stripped them. And the reason is evident. We have not let the Holy Spirit have His way with our inner life. Had the sap of His presence been mightily within us, we should have been laden with luscious fruitage; it would have been impossible to be otherwise.

Do you lack *power for service?* You have no burning thirst for the salvation

of others. You are not on fire for souls.
You have never been in agony over the
alienation of men from God. And when
you speak, there is no power in what
you say. The devils laugh at your attempts to exorcise them. The sleeper
turns for a moment uneasily; but soon
falls into profounder slumber than ever.
The home, the class, the congregation,
yield no results. No hand-picked fruit
fills your basket. No finny shoal breaks
your nets. No recruits accept your call
to arms. And you cannot expect it to
be otherwise till you obtain the power
which our Lord promised when He said,
"Ye shall receive the power of the Holy
Ghost coming upon you." It was when
the early Christians were filled with the
Holy Ghost, that they spake the word of
God with boldness; and gave witness
with great power to the resurrection of
the Lord Jesus.

These and many other deficiencies
would be met, if only we were filled with

the Holy Spirit. There would be a joy, a power, a consciousness of the presence of the Lord Jesus, an habitual rest in the will of God, which would be a joyful discovery to us; if only we refused to be satisfied with anything less than the full indwelling of the Holy Spirit.

Entire consecration to the service of the Lord Jesus is a great step in advance of the experience of most Christians; but even that is not enough. It is often largely *negative*; but we require something strongly *positive*, to meet the necessities of our hearts and of our times. And this is to be sought in our entire possesion by that mighty Spirit, whose advent at Pentecost has dated a new era for the Church and the world.

Of course He was always in the world. It was the Holy Spirit of Pentecost who brooded over chaos; and spoke in prophets and holy men; and nerved the heroes and saints of Old Testament time. The day of Pentecost did not introduce a new Spirit into the world; but inaugurated an era in which the weakest and meanest of the saints might possess Him in the same measure as they did who lived upon its farther side. Before that momentous day His fulness was the prerogative of only the few, the *elite*, the Elijahs, and Isaiahs, and Daniels; but since that day He has been shed forth in all His plenitude on the many—on women and children; on obscure thinkers and hidden workers; on handmaids and servants; on all and any who were prepared to fulfil the conditions, and to abide by the results. Why not on us?

We are willing to admit that the special gifts of the Holy Ghost belong to the Apostolic age. Given for a specific purpose, they are now withdrawn; though it is a serious question whether they might not have been continued, if only the Church had been more faithful to her sacred trust.

But the special gifts of the Holy Ghost

are altogether apart from His blessed
fulness. That is not the exclusive right
of any age. Confined to no limited area
or epoch in the history of the Church, it
pours its tides of light and power around
us, as the Nile in flood; nor is there a
single plot of garden-ground, however
remote, into which it will not come, to
fertilize and enrich, if only the channel
of communication be kept cleansed
and open.

"Be filled with the Spirit" is an in-
junction as wide-reaching in its demands
as "Husbands, love your wives," which
is found on the same page. It is a positive command, which we must obey at
our peril; and all God's commands are
enablings. In other words, He is prepared to make us what He tells us to
become. Moreover, on the day of Pentecost, in words which are the charta of our
right to the fulness of the Holy Spirit, the
Apostle Peter told the listening crowds
that the fulness which had suddenly come

on them from the ascended Lord— and which was a direct fulfilment of ancient prophecy—was not for them only, or for their children; but for as many as were afar off, even for them whom the Lord God should call. Are you one of His called ones? Then rejoice! because that fulness is for you. Be not faithless, but believing! Lay claim at once to the covenanted portion; and thank God for having cast your lot in an age of such marvellous possibilities.

I. Excite holy desire by considering what the Fulness of the Spirit means.

We cannot expect to have it, if we are quite content to live without it. Our Father is not likely to entrust this priceless gift to those who are indifferent to its possession. Where the flame of desire burns low, there can be no intelligent expectation that the Holy Spirit's fulness shall be realized.

And it is not enough to have a fitful

and inconstant desire, which flames up to-day, but will remain dormant for months and years. There must be a steady purpose, able to stand the test of waiting, if need be, for ten days; and to bear the rebuff of silence or apparent denial.

And yet the flame of desire needs fuel. We must muse before that fire can burn. And it becomes us, therefore, to stir up the gift that is within us, by a quiet consideration of all that is meant by becoming Spirit-filled.

There is no book which will so move us in this direction as the Acts of the Apostles. It is perfectly marvellous to see what this fulness did for those who first received it. Cowards became brave. Obtuse intellects, which had stumbled at the simplest truths, suddenly awoke to apprehend the Master's scheme. Such power attended their words that crowds became congregations; Christ's murderers became His worshippers and friends;

councils of clever men were not able to withstand the simple eloquence of indisputable facts; towns and countries were shaken, and yielded converts by the thousand to the unlearned but fervid preachers of the cross.

And all this was simply attributable to the power which had become the common property of the whole Church. And there is not a fragment of reason why it should not do so much for us. And, as we contrast that triumphant success to our halting progress, shall not we be filled with uncontrollable longings that He should work similar results by us?

We may still further secure the same results by studying the biography of saintly men belonging to recent centuries. Happy the man within reach of a library, the shelves of which are well lined with books of holy biography. He will never, never be in want of additional stimulus as he reads the story of McCheyne and W. C. Burns, of Brainard and Martyn, of

Jonathan Edwards and D. L. Moody. He will not envy or repine; but he will constantly lift eye and heart to Heaven, asking that as much may be done through himself.

And moreover, the promises of the Scripture are enough to incite us to the uttermost. That rivers of water should flow from us; that we should never need to be anxious about our words, because they would be given; that we should be taught all things, and led into the whole circle of truth; that we should know Christ, and be changed into His image; that we should have power—all this is so fascinating, that it is impossible not to glow with a holy desire to be charged with the Holy Spirit, as a jar with electricity. And, if needs be, we shall be prepared to bear the test of long waiting, as the faithful few did in the upper room.

II. Seek this blessed Fulness from the right Motive.

God will not find water for us to use

for turning our own water-wheels. He will do nothing to minister to our pride. He will not give us the Holy Spirit to enable us to gain celebrity; or to procure a name; or to live an easy, self-contented life.

If we seek the Holy Spirit merely for our happiness, or comfort, or liberty of soul, it will be exceedingly unlikely that He will be given. His one passion is— the glory of the Lord Jesus; and He can only make His abode with those who are willing to be at one with Him in this. "Can two walk together except they be agreed?" But if you are actuated simply by the desire that the Lord Jesus may be magnified in you, whether by life or death; if you long, above all, that men should turn away from you to Him, as they did from John the Baptist —then rejoice, because you are near blessing beyond words to describe. If your motives fall below this standard, trust in Him to enlighten and purify

them, and offer Him a free entrance
within. It will not then be long ere
there shall be a gracious response; and
the Lord, whom ye seek, shall suddenly
come to His temple, and He shall sit as
a refiner of silver, that the sons of Levi
may offer an offering in righteousness.

III. Consider that Holy Scripture is
    His special Organ.

A subtle danger besets the teaching
of this most helpful doctrine, and one
that we need to guard against. Some
earnest people have magnified the inner
light and leading of the Holy Spirit to
the neglect of the Word which He gave,
and through which He still works on
human hearts. This is a great mistake,
and the prolific parent of all kinds
of evil. For directly we put aside
the Word of God, we lay ourselves open
to the solicitation of the many voices
that speak within our hearts; and we
have no test, no criterion of truth, no

standard of appeal. How can we know the Spirit of God, in some of the more intricate cases which are brought into the court of conscience, unless our judgment is deeply imbued with the Word of God?

We must not be content with the Spirit without the Word; or with the Word without the Spirit. Our life must travel along these two, as the locomotive along the parallel metals. The word is the chosen organ of the Spirit; and it is only by our devout contact with it that we shall be enabled to detect His voice. It is by the Word that the Spirit will enter our hearts, as the heat of the sun passes into our chambers through the beams of light that enter the open casement.

We need a widespread revival of Bible study. These mines of Scripture, lying beneath the surface, call loudly for investigation and discovery: and those who shall obey the appeal, and set themselves to the devout and laborious study

of the inner meaning of the Word, shall
be soon aware that they have received
the filling that they seek.

IV. Be prepared to let the Holy
Ghost do as He will with you.

The Holy Ghost is in us, and by this
means Christ is in us; for He dwells in
us by the Spirit, as the sun dwells in the
world by means of the atmosphere vi-
brating with waves of light. But we must
perpetually yield to Him, as water to the
containing vessel. This is not easy; indeed it can only be accomplished by
incessant self-judgment, and the perpetual mortification of our own self-life.

What is our position before God in this
respect? We have chosen Jesus as our
substitute; but have we also chosen
Him, by the Holy Spirit, as our Life?
Can we say, like the Apostle: "Not
I, but Christ liveth in me"? If so, we
must be prepared for all that it involves.
We must be willing for the principle of

the new life to grow at the expense of the self-life. We must consent for the one to increase, whilst the other decreases, through processes which are painful enough to the flesh. Nay, we must ourselves be ever on the alert, hastening the processes of judgment, condemnation, and crucifixion. We must keep true in our allegiance to the least behest of the Holy Spirit, though it cost tears of blood.

The perpetual filling of the Holy Spirit is only possible to those who obey Him; and who obey Him in all things. There is nothing trivial in this life. By the neglect of slight commands, a soul may speedily get out of the sunlit circle, and lose the gracious plenitude of Spirit-power. A look, a word, a refusal, may suffice to grieve Him in ourselves, and to quench Him in others. Count the cost; yet do not shrink back afraid of what He may demand. He is the Spirit of love; and He loves us too well to cause grief, unless there is a reason, which we should approve, if we knew as much as He.

V.   RECEIVE HIM BY FAITH.

"As ye have received Christ Jesus the Lord, so walk ye in Him."   Faith is the one law of the Divine household.   And as once you obtained forgiveness and salvation by faith, so now claim and receive the Holy Spirit's fulness.

Fulfil the conditions already named; wait quietly but definitely before God in prayer, for He gives His Holy Spirit *to them that ask Him:* then reverently appropriate this glorious gift; and rise from your knees, and go on your way, reckoning that God has kept His word, and that you are filled with the Spirit. Trust Him day by day to fill you and keep you filled.   According to your faith, so shall it be done to you.

There may not be, at first, the sound of rushing wind, or the coronet of fire, or the sensible feeling of His presence. Do not look for these, any more than the young convert should look to feeling as an evidence of acceptance. But believe, in spite of feeling, that you are filled. Say over and over, "I thank Thee, O my God, that Thou hast kept Thy word with me. I opened my mouth, and Thou hast filled it; though, as yet, I am not aware of any special change." And the feeling will sooner or later break in upon your consciousness, and you will rejoice with exceeding great joy; and all the fruits of the Spirit will begin to show themselves.

There is, of course, more in the doctrine of the Holy Spirit than is at all realized by the writer of these feeble lines. The fiery baptism of the Holy Spirit may be something far beyond. Let us not then be content to miss anything possible to redeemed men; but, leaving the things that are behind, let us press on to those before, striving to apprehend all for

which we have been apprehended by
Christ Jesus. And if we persevere, we
shall realize possibilities in our lives that
shall recall the days of the Apostles, and
enable us to understand what Jesus
meant when He spoke of those greater
works which should be wrought by them
that should believe in Him after He had
gone to His Father.

VIII.

Our Work for Christ.

"To every man his work."—*Mark xiii. 34.*

THE Christian life is sure to manifest itself in holy activity; as certainly as the life of a vegetable or plant manifests itself in flower and fruit. It is perfectly true to speak of such activities as *work* —"to every man his work." But to describe them as *fruit*, brings out another shade of meaning, and indicates our entire dependence for all successful work, on our living connection with our glorious Lord.

The Lord Jesus is Himself the great Worker. He came to finish the work which His Father gave Him to do. St. Mark fitly describes Him during His earthly career as the swift and incessant worker, whose days were crowded with incident from early dawn far on into the night. "I must work the works of Him that sent Me, while it is day."

It is a great mistake to suppose that His work has ceased. The Gospels tell us only of what He *began* to do and teach. But the book of the Acts of the Apostles, which might be better called the Book of the Acts of the living and ascended Lord, takes up the wondrous story, and tells us of what He continued to do and teach, after He had passed through the heavens to the right hand of God. He is still the great Worker throughout all the ages, both in the universe, and in the Church. And the sacred record already mentioned closes abruptly with great fitness; because the wondrous story of the Acts of the Lord did not finish when Paul in his hired house, for two whole years, had preached unhindered the things concerning the Kingdom of God, in the metropolis of the world-kingdom. It runs on throughout the centuries, and is still being written by angel fingers in the chronicles of eternity.

But is it not true that the ascended Lord requires organs and instruments for the expression and working out of His mighty thoughts and purposes? He is the Head of the body, the Church; and He needs members, as the medium through which He may convey His purposes of grace and power towards the world. As of old He passed the blessings that throbbed in His heart through the hands, and lips, and presence of His mortal body; so now He must employ His own beloved ones to be His hands, His lips, His feet, His body—by which men may receive healing virtue. St. Paul was therefore consistent with the deepest truth, when "he declared particularly what things God *had wrought* among the Gentiles by his ministry." And we shall work effectively when we understand that we are not required to originate or execute work *for* Christ, so much as to work out His schemes, in His own strength.

Who amongst the readers of these lines does not long to be as useful as possible in this brief life; to fulfil all the possibilities of usefulness; and to apprehend that for which Christ has apprehended him? But this can never be, until all the powers of nature, which Christ has redeemed, are placed absolutely at His disposal, with this prayer, "Do with me, in me, to me, by me, as Thou wilt; only make as much of me as can be made on this side of the gates of pearl. Work out Thine own ideal. Fulfil in me all the good pleasure of Thy will. Perfect that which concerneth me."

The maker of the organ can best develop the sweet and mighty tones which sleep within its compass. The inventor of an ingenious machine can best unfold its varied appliances. And surely it stands to reason that He who knows what is in us can best call forth our faculties, and use them, and manipulate them for His glory, and to our joy. Oh, what could not the Lord Jesus do by us, if only we were wholly yielded to Him!

Let us note a few hints which may be of assistance to Christian workers.

I. Work from Pure Motives.

Legends tell that when the Emperor Justinian had built the Byzantine Church with a view to his own aggrandisement and glory, on the day of dedication he looked in vain for his own name on the memorial stone. Angel hands had obliterated it, and substituted for it that of the widow, Euphrasia—whose only merit was, that out of pure devotion she had strewn a little straw in front of the beasts that drew the heavily-laden trucks of marble from the quarry to the sacred pile. His motive was so ignoble that heaven ignored his gift; hers was so pure and lovely that she received credit for the whole.

Alas! how much of our work vanishes, without note in heaven, because it springs from no motive that can pass muster there. Earth rings with its fame, and therein we find our only and sufficient recompense; but the tidings never travel further, whilst other deeds, which arrest no notice here, stir all heaven with interest and wonder, because of the mighty motives that gave them birth.

With what shame do many of us review the ignoble and worthless motives by which we have been prompted. To gain a livelihood; to win a name; to excite applause; to outvie some neighbor; to win a victory; to accomplish a difficult and almost impossible task; these have inspired us in many deeds of Christian service, which have received the commendation of those who judge by appearance, and not by heart. How could our God be pleased with us, or accept our service! Our most splendid deeds have been irreparably spoilt by the meanness of the motives that prompted them.

Our motives must be pure. The root will affect all the fruit. The stream can-

not rise higher than its source. We must
get rid of the constant thought of self.
We must become oblivious to the praise
or blame of man. We must let the sun
of Divine love burn out the fires of self-
ish ambition and personal aims. We
must bring our weak and weary hearts
to the Heart-physician, asking Him to
cleanse them by the inspiration of His
Holy Spirit, disentwining the clinging
evil of self, and filling us with His own
sweet, ingenuous, and perfect love. May
our hearts burn with the pure flame of
devotion that trembles in the hearts of
seraphs! This our cry in life and death:
"Glory to God in the Highest!"

II. WORK ON GOD'S PLAN.

One of the most suggestive texts in
the Bible, far-reaching in its many ap-
plications, is that in which God says to
Moses, "See that thou make all things
according to the pattern showed thee in
the Mount." Not a stake, or a curtain,
or an atom of fragrant spice was left to

the genius of the artificer, or the fancy of the lawgiver. All was unfolded to Moses in elaborate detail; and all he had to do was to produce that plan in careful and exact obedience, until at last it stood complete before the wondering host of Israel. And God provided the material in abundance, out of which the plan was to be elaborated. If we will execute His plans, we need have no anxiety about the stuff; He will make Himself responsible for that.

Does not this touch the secret of much of our failure? We reason thus: "This seems a feasible thing; it promises well; other men are doing it; success seems within grasp, and would be very sweet: I shall certainly go in for it." We do not stay to ask whether it is one of those good works which God has before prepared for us to walk in. We do not seek to know, by prayer and waiting, whether it is in God's plan for us. We do not humbly wait to be taught if God wants our help in this special direction. And it is only when we have plunged deeply into our course, and have met with all manner of discouragement, that we begin to question whether we should have adopted it at all. Then we run to ask God to extricate us; to help us out; and to forgive us for having built, and launched, and chartered our ships, without asking Him if we were acting in accordance with His will.

The fact is, *we* start an enterprise, and presently ask God to help us; instead of first asking what He was doing, and whether we could help Him.

Do not think that this mode of life will lead to listless dreaming. None are so energetic, so swift, so mighty in their holy activities as those who know that they are on God's lines; doing their little bit in the mighty scheme of tesselated pavement; sure that His accomplished plan will amply justify them; and casting all responsibilities on His perfect wisdom.

Do not run hither and thither, asking for work. How can any one tell you what the Master wants you to do? We can but guess at the best. Go straight to the Lord Jesus for yourselves. Tell Him you cannot bear to be shut out of His glorious fellowship. Entreat Him to indicate your place. And never rest content until, like Peter, you turn from the vision to the task; and, in the knock of the far-travelled messengers, you are summoned to the work which needs you.

III. WORK AS THOSE FRESHLY CLEANSED.

The priests must wash in the laver before they perform the service of the Sanctuary. They must be clean who bear the vessels of the Lord. A man must purge himself from iniquity, if he shall be "a vessel unto honor, sanctified and meet for the Master's use, and prepared unto every good work." (2 Tim. ii. 21.)

If, in haste, we would give a draught of refreshing water to a traveller, we take from our shelf the first vessel which is *clean.* We pass over the elegant and richly-chased cup for the earthenware mug, if the latter has a cleanliness which the former lacks. And our Lord Jesus will gladly use us for His service, though we be of but common ware, if only we are clean and ready for use.

In our hospitals, the instruments used in operations are constantly kept in carbolic acid, that they may not carry the slightest contagion to the open wound; and we cannot touch the open and festering wounds which sin has caused without injury to ourselves and others, unless we are ever in the flow of the blood and water of which St. John speaks.

IV. WORK IN GOD'S STRENGTH.

No man is sent to the warfare on his own charges; and yet many Christians argue as if that were one of heaven's standing orders. None, however, are ever called to a work which God does not know is within the limits of the strength which He has given, or which

He is ready to give, to the opened, up-
turned heart. He does not want our
strength—it is often a hindrance to
Him; because we are so apt to rely on
it, to the exclusion of Himself. He wants
our weakness, our infirmities, our noth-
ingness—"that the excellency of the
power may be of God, and not of us."
So far from your consciousness of power-
lessness being a barrier to your efficient
work, it will be one of the strongest elements in your success—if only you are
driven to lay hold on His strength, and
be at peace. "My grace is sufficient for
thee: for my strength is made perfect in
weakness. Most gladly, therefore, will
I rather glory in my infirmities, that the
power of Christ may rest upon me."

When asking Christians to undertake
certain branches of Christian work, one
is so often met with the excuse, "I cannot do it; I am not fitted for it. I have
no power to speak." Such have much
need to get back to the desert and learn

the significant lesson of the rod which
Moses held in his hand. He was questioning his sufficiency to take up the
work which was being thrust upon him;
but he learnt that if only a rod is cast
down before God, it becomes endowed
with new powers; it can be and do what
would be impossible by nature: and
through the power of God it may become
invested with such might as to carve a
way through the waves; roll back the
hosts of Amalek; and bring water from
the flinty rock. Why should not we be
as that rod in the hands of ·Christ?
Without Him we cannot be other than
broken reeds; but in and with Him we
become pillars in the temple from which
we shall go no more out. "I can do all
things in Him which strengtheneth me."

And there is no way so good of getting
God's strength as being diligent students
of His precious Word. This is the medium of conveying strength to our inmost
souls; as the grain conveys the strength

of the earth to the nutriment of our natural life. Read your Bibles, Christian workers, if you would be strong. And it also stands to reason that the Holy Ghost is much more likely to use marvellously the man whose mind is steeped and saturated with the thoughts and phraseology of Scripture, which has been indited by Him as the medium of eternal truths to human hearts.

V. Work in Believing Expectancy.

How often and how truly it has been said that God never uses a discouraged man. No great measure of success will ever come to him who does not believe in it, and expect it. In this, as in all other spiritual work, we are governed by one unchanging law: According to your faith be it done unto you. "Only be thou strong and very courageous."

And why should we not go forth with the elastic tread of those who know that they shall doubtless come again with rejoicing, bringing with them their sheaves? We go on God's errands; we are provided with His seed, we are directed by His unerring wisdom to our plot in the field; we are sure of His co-operation in giving sun and shower, dew and rain. We may have to wait, as all true husbandmen must; but there can be no doubt as to the ultimate issue.

Oh, what a glorious work is ours! To give effect to the yearnings of Divine love; to be the organs and instruments of the redemptive purpose of God; to be associated with Christ in the salvation of the lost; to pluck men as brands from the burning, and to hold them aloft as torches for the progress of the King; to hasten the glad day of His second coming; to be His heralds and ambassadors—these were enough to lure an archangel from his seat. Well is it to have been summoned to do it; and a thousand times better to know that it is to be the employment of eternal ages, of which it is written, "His servants shall serve Him.

IX.

Concluding Words.

"Keep yourselves in the love of God."—Jude 21.

THE longer we live, the less we care to speak of our love to God, and the more we dwell on God's love to us. As we climb the hill of Christian experience, we see the ever-growing horizon of the ocean of divine tenderness; and we become ashamed even to mention the pool of our love that lies far away in the vale beneath. Besides, we come to see that all true love to God is only a reflected gleam of His great love towards us. "We love Him because He first loved us."

There is no sweeter atmosphere in which to live than the perpetual consciousness that God loves us. Like the steady heat of the hot-house producing flowers and fruits amid the frosts of December: so, in this icy world, the genial

glow of the love of God experienced per-
ennially by the believer will produce
those results which are exotics to this
World, though they are native to the
soil of the New Jerusalem.

When the Apostle bids us keep ourselves in the love of God, he surely does
not mean that we need to exert ourselves
to prevent the cessation of God's love toward us.   The love of God is without
variableness, or shadow of turning. Having loved His own which are in the world,
He loves them unto the end.   We may
rest satisfied that nothing can separate
us from the love of God, which is in Jesus
Christ our Lord.   If we are faithless, He
remaineth faithful.   If we wander away
into backsliding and coldness, He con-
tinues immutably the same. If we, like
Peter, deny Him, yet He still looks on
us with yearning affection, enough to
break our hearts.   Oh, clasp this blessed
thought to your inner consciousness! —
that the love of God is more tenacious

than a mother's—"she may forget"—
and more lasting than hills or mountains, which "may depart."

But the love of God to us is one thing;
and our appreciation and enjoyment of
that love is quite another. The one is
unalterably the same; while the other
is fitful and intermittent. Sometimes
we are very sensible of the warm beam
of God's love shining blessedly into our
souls; at other times we have no such
joyous consciousness of His love: but
we must remember that God's love to
us does not in any way depend on our
consciousness of it. It is not most, because we happen to feel it most; or least,
because we have almost ceased to feel it
at all. The one is no guage of the amount
of the other. God's love to us is ever
constant, however much our appreciation of it may vary. When the sunlight
beams seem to touch only a rim of the
moon's surface, we do not argue that the
sun is growing cold and dark. When a

child wanders far afield from home and mother, we do not suppose that the love has necessarily died out in that mother's heart.

Nevertheless, though our consciousness of God's love, does not determine its amount or constancy, yet it is very delightful and helpful to realize it always. Thus we become most sensitive to sin. Thus we acquire purity of heart. Thus we become strong and fearless. Thus, too, we become magnetic, attracting others to Him who has made us what we are.

This then is the question with which we opened, and with which we close, these thoughts on Christian Living—"May we not live in the hourly consciousness of the love of God toward us.

Is not this what Jesus meant when He said, "I have kept My Father's commandments, and *abide* in His love?" Is not this what He meant, when He bade us keep His commandments and abide in His own love? And what else did Jude mean by bidding his fellow-Christians to keep themselves "in the love of God"?

We may not always or exclusively be dwelling on it; but continually looking up from our work, and finding that that benignant face is still smiling on us; and that that over-arching heaven of love is still above and around; not able to speak much of our love to God, but always able to speak of His love to us—like a child who plays about the house without questioning for a moment, because it feels instinctively that all around it is shining the love of the mother.

There are three or four brief hints that may be of service:—

I. Take time to consider God's love to you. God loves the world, because He loves each unit in the great sum of human life. We see the parterres of spring; to Him each flower is distinct. To us the sparrows are so similar that we cannot distinguish one from the rest; but He marks each sparrow's fall. We stand in wonder beneath the arch of the starry sky, and are bewildered by the multitudinousness of the star-dust. He calls each atom by its separate name. And so when we think of God's love to us, we must not think He loves us as part of the race; but with a special individualizing love, which singles us out of the crowd, as a father loves each child with a love in which no other can share.

"Thou art as much His care, as if beside
Nor man, nor angel lived in heaven and earth."

This belief in God's personal love is very helpful. It prevents us from feeling lost in a crowd. But it is not natural or easy at first. We must be patient, and take time to allow the thought to possess us, in its mighty grasp. We must get alone, and shut the door upon the busy world, and set ourselves to comprehend the meaning of those three small words, *God loves me*. We must learn that it is of the very nature of an Infinite Being to be as much in one place as though He were in no other place; and to love one lonely heart as if there were none other to share His love in all the wide universe. In the morning, before you enter on the calls of daily duty, take time — five minutes — quietly to realize that you are the object of the deep personal love of the Infinite God.

II. Accept all the incidents of the day as coming from His love. I do not see how we can make distinctions between God's ordaining and His permissive providence, any more than we can between His special and general providence. All life, and its many incidents; what comes to us directly from His hand, equally with what is permitted to happen to us through the means of others — must be traced back to Himself as the ultimate final cause. Our Lord was delivered by the determinate counsel and fore-knowledge of God; though this did not lessen the wickedness of the hands by which He was crucified and slain. Here is the mystery of the ages; but let not the mystery rob us of the undoubted truth, that God is behind all events.

And God is love. All events, therefore, must be consistent with His love. And we must recognize this, if we would keep ourselves in its glad and constant enjoyment. When any bright thing befalls you; when any one says anything kind of you; when an unexpected gift falls at your feet; when a new friendship enters your life; when the sun shines brightly on your path—look up, and know that all lovely and helpful things are the children of the love of God. Do not be so occupied with the gift, or the channel through which it comes, as to ignore the Giver Himself.

And when unkind things are said or done; when robber bands steal your goods, as Job's; when friends disappoint you, and Shimeis curse—then look up, and be sure that all is permitted by a love that cares for you none the less tenderly when it withholds its help. "Jesus loved

Martha, and her sister, and Lazarus:
when He heard, *therefore*, that he was
sick, He abode two days still in the same
place where He was."

Thus every event that comes to you
will link you, by a golden clasp, with
the love of God.

III. Be channels of God's love to others.
In the spring, the vine-root, bursting with
life-power, longs for branches through
which it may pour its tides of life forth
to refresh thirsty souls; and surely the
love of God is ever seeking for kindred
hearts, who shall be channels of
communication with the world. The
world, too, needs love. There is nothing
which can slake its thirst, but the love
of God. It will ever thirst again till it
drinks of that stream.

Why should not you, my reader, be one
of the channels through which God's
love may pour itself out to refresh him
that is weary? If you are willing, you will
find yourself beginning to care for men
as never before; and there will be a new

power of affection opened within you, which shall betray its Divine origin.

And what, think you, shall be the effect of this upon yourself, except to teach you the meaning of God's love to *you*? For the water which flows along a channel can refresh the flowerets that grow upon its banks. Those that live in love to others know the love of God to themselves; and to keep other men in our love is to keep ourselves in the love of God. Forsake wrath, jealousy, and envy, in the power of God's grace, and learn the new, glad lesson of love.

IV. Associate with those who love God. No one of us can know the fulness of God's love in the loneliness of our own communings. We need to associate *with all saints* to learn its height and depth, and length and breadth. It is a mistake to isolate ourselves from communion with Christians, or from corporate Church-life; and it is my earnest advice to all young Christians, as to all secret disciples, to find some happy centre of Christian fellowship, and join it.

We see the love of God from different angles. It shines on us with different hues. And no one can fully appreciate it, and its full extent, who has not spoken with other Christians about it, and tried to catch some new beauty in their conceptions. Talk much of the love of God to those around you. Hear them, and ask them questions. So shall your heart burn within you, and Jesus will make Himself known in some deeper, sweeter guise. Christian converse is a great help towards the abiding realization of the love of God.

V. Live in obedience to every known command. "If ye keep My commandments, ye shall abide in My love; as I have kept My Father's commandments, and abide in His love." This is the secret— to search the Word to see if you are keeping all His commands; to seek and keep His laws; to put the government upon His shoulders; to do His will, at whatever cost to self-will; to obey, not to win aught from His hand, but just to please Him; to ask forgiveness and restoration if you have erred or gone astray. Here is the essential condition of walking in the light of His love.

Who has not been conscious of a sweet manifestation of love, when some difficult duty has been done for His dear sake alone? As when Jesus was baptized, the heavens were opened, and the voice of God declared Him to be His beloved Son.

Let us "walk in the light, as He is in the light": so shall we be conscious not of light only, but of love.

There is no need for us to live in a cold and arctic zone, if only we fulfil the conditions here set down. We may not always be equally buoyant, or equally exuberant; or equally responsive; but we shall never lose the bright glad consciousness that we are loved by the Love that spared not the only-begotten Son.